WRITE YOUR DANG BOOK!

A CHEERLEADING, TOUGH-LOVE
COMPANION
FOR FIRST-TIME
NONFICTION WRITERS

MICHELLE A. VANDEPAS

Edited by: Laurie Knight
Cover Design by: Kristina Edstrom

EMP⊙WER
P   R   E   S   S

An Imprint for GracePoint Publishing (www.GracePointPublishing.com)

GracePoint Matrix, LLC
624 S. Cascade Ave, Suite 201
Colorado Springs, CO 80903
www.GracePointMatrix.com
Email: Admin@GracePointMatrix.com
SAN # 991-6032

A Library of Congress Control Number has been requested and is pending.

ISBN: (Paperback) 978-1-968891-05-3
eISBN: 978-1-968891-06-0

Books may be purchased for educational, business, or sales promotional use.
For non-retail bulk order requests contact Orders@GracePointPublishing.com

Printed in U.S.A

Endorsements

Michelle is an amazing empowered leader within publishing who is a master at sharing her knowledge to empower everyone to find the book within.

~ *Beth*

I'm so grateful to Michelle for helping me get my first book contract with a prestigious publisher! Since I was a little girl, I have always wanted to publish a book. Michelle helped me write a very professional book proposal with a clickable table of contents. She helped me write the parts of the proposal that I had no experience with—the pitch, the market, competing books, intended audience, delivery details, and author promotion. Once an editor became interested in the proposal, she helped me correspond and negotiate with her. Thanks to Michelle, my lifelong dream of publishing is coming true!

~ *Julia*

You gave me the vision that what I dreamed for my book was not only feasible but doable. I was afraid my dream was too big considering my age. You convinced me otherwise… thank you.

~ *Gwen*

I dubbed Michelle the book whisperer many years ago. Since that time she's helped me with several books. Thank you Michelle!

~ *Sarah*

Check out our site at:
www.GracePointPublishing.com

Table of Contents

Section I:
Mindset

Section II:
Time to Get to Writing

Afterthoughts

Section I
Mindset

Note from Michelle

"Do not let your book die inside of you."

That is my mantra, my dream, and my wish for you.

Your book, your voice, your message, they all matter.

If you are like me, you have a message and know that the world, humanity, and society can benefit from hearing it. You know you need a platform or a way to share your message and have an inkling: *I can write a book!* You may never get started, or at the very least, you write a page or two, or fifty, and suddenly, you have no idea how to put one more word on the page.

Or you have been writing for months, years, or decades and find that your pieces are disjointed and have incoherent themes. Each time you recommit to writing, you get over-whelmed or stuck, and self-doubt creeps in, leading to more delays. Then you feel bad about the writing and start to doubt and self-sabotage, and the book never gets written.

You've probably talked about your ideas for hours. But when you face the keyboard and an empty screen, your thoughts stop—or jam up like six lanes of rush-hour traffic. That's writer's block.

Maybe you've taken voice notes, filled your phone with thoughts, carried note cards in your pocket, or started a blog or YouTube channel you meant to transcribe someday.

You've built an audience and shared your message, but the longer the book stays unfinished, the more it haunts you.

The intention is there. The result? Not yet.

There are countless ways your book has been delayed, and yet you still feel *called* to write. Self-doubt, distraction, fear, overwhelm, and countless other inner saboteurs have spoken up, and you *still* have that deep desire niggling at you.

Please know this: You are not alone.

This book is for anyone who feels the call to write. It's for those who find themselves stuck, whether they're struggling to find the right words, battling self-doubt, or worrying about how the book will be received. If you've ever felt uncertain about your ability to bring your ideas to life, this book is here to guide, encourage, and help you move forward with confidence.

Over the past quarter century, I've collaborated with clients who have dreamed for years, sometimes decades, about writing their books but life has stopped them. Family, time, work, and health constraints are real. Life happens. But even with all that, your book still matters. What other choice is there? While this may be true for you, you've got great intentions. What I've come to realize, what I've come to know deep in my heart, is that these are all excuses. You've picked up this book and it's your time. Now.

The truth is that some people write, and some don't. Some people have a book inside them, and some don't. Before you get mad at me, you must know I've been writing *this* book (and my next, legacy book) for almost a decade. I wrote a chapter, put it aside, and started again. I've started and stopped when I found myself going down varying rabbit holes thinking, *That's not it.*

Sure, all my ideas are there, and then when I start gathering them up and stringing them together, life happens. Like you, health, family, and work have all gotten in the way. And the most challenging part about staying with it all is that I don't consider myself a writer. Yep. I'm not a writer (there's a whole chapter coming about this), so I deeply and intimately understand you.

We procrastinate for lots of reasons: fear, overwhelm, or sometimes timing. In my TEDx talk, I explore the line between procrastination and percolation and the idea that it's just not time yet. We've got to think about what's next before we act. We need more context, or we have obligations and must take care of our ailing neighbor. But when it's time, it's time, and the feeling will just keep nagging until you act. And then it *is* time.

In all the years I've coached and coaxed books out of clients and upcoming authors, these are a few of the top reasons I've found that people stop writing (or never even begin). They ask themselves:

- Who am I to write?
- Hasn't it all been said before anyway?
- Maybe I don't have anything new to say?
- What if I publish and no one buys the book?

These are excuses. They stop you from expressing yourself. They create a loop in your brain that makes you stop and start, stop, and start.

How can you get out of this loop? Know that you aren't alone, you aren't broken, and you aren't unworthy. You are worthy. You have the right to speak your mind, write your words, and be heard just because you have something to say.

As a publisher, I know even the most prolific and accomplished writers get stuck in their heads, circling around and around with their words. I've looked inside at how authors get

3

past their own self-doubt and how new authors get moving. And it's not always what you might think.

Yes, some of moving ahead comes with support in editing, and knowing you have a team behind you, and it's also just getting words onto paper.

Just do it. You don't need to plan how the book will look yet. Focus only on getting words out. Everything else comes later.

There are so many types of publishing: self, hybrid, traditional, trade/hybrid, blogging, and many more. You may not know the differences yet or which way to go. You mustn't get caught up on how to publish, who will read it, or if you will sell any books—there's plenty of time for that later, because guess what, none of that matters if you don't write the book.

You've got to write your book. It seems so obvious. Yet, it's the most challenging part of the whole process. There is no bypass (although some hacks are coming).

When you finish your first draft, you'll be surprised by how much creativity and self-reflection show up. A great book asks you to dig deep, and while the process can be fun, it's also frustrating, rewarding, and challenging. And yet, it's one of the most fulfilling things you'll ever do.

Getting your words on paper and putting yourself out there is scary. It can feel like sitting naked in front of the world, especially if your book is personal. Are you telling stories about your life and your transformation? Have you studied different schools of thought in healing, self-development, or nutrition and synthesized them into your own system? Are you ready to share it? When you start thinking outside the box that everyone else accepts, you're risking your reputation, name, business, and so much more by publishing your ideas. Do you really want to do that?

Yes, it's scary. And yes, it's worth it.

What if you have the exact process that others need right now? What if your new approach to an old concept sparks something that changes *everything* for the best? What if your contribution moves the needle just a little bit toward a greater humanity?

What if you write the book and no one cares, or those who read it hate it? Yikes! Then what?

Or, what if you write this and everyone needs and loves it?

Writing is vulnerable. It's not easy. But if you keep going and push through the hard parts, finishing your draft will be one of the most rewarding things you've ever done. As you write down your thoughts, you will learn and grow into embracing who you already are. You will stretch and question and wonder. You'll have heartfelt thoughts you've never said aloud that fit perfectly on the page.

The writing process often helps you discover your voice and message more clearly than before. It emerges as you show up for the page

You might find yourself writing words you were unaware of—channeling another voice or another part of yourself. Some call that *inspired writing* where you have accessed your highest self, your soul, or God. Whatever you might call this other voice, I implore you to listen, to tap into the wisest, highest version of your soul so you can share yourself with the world.

After all, that is your purpose: to share yourself and your love with the world.

Intro

Now that your heart is ready, let's walk through the practical steps, because the writing journey is both soulful and structured. You've picked up this book, so I'm presuming you are writing or thinking of writing your nonfiction book. Your story, a memoir perhaps, or a teaching or healing book. Maybe it's another type of nonfiction book that will help humanity in some way. It might be your one and only legacy book, leaving your imprint on the world, acknowledging the talents and strengths you've developed along the way. Whatever you are writing, you are in the right place. This book will help and support your author journey.

My dream for you is that you'll be excited to start and finish your first draft by the end of this book. I hope you will take advantage of some of the videos and extra bonus content on my website to help you get moving and avoid procrastination. You'll find the links in the back of this book. But above all else, I hope you will write.

I'm going to take you through what has worked for my clients when I have been a book coach and what has worked for my authors when I have been their publisher. You'll learn how to find your voice, your readers, and who needs to read your book. These aren't just steps—they're turning points that help authors move from uncertainty to completion and they will help you create a vision for your book.

- Why you're writing your book and its purpose (for your reader and yourself).
- How to outline your book.
- Writing your first draft (and what's included in that).
- What mistakes authors make and how not to make those!
- Great writing hacks.
- Then your next steps.

I'll ask you to dig deep into your subconscious, your creative magic, and trust that you have the answers, the wisdom, and the strength to finish your book.

You can do this, but you only need to scroll through social media to see all the memes about how hard writing is or how self-doubt permeates the process, and you likely have seen the constant advice to just keep going. The Ernest Hemingway avatar of the tortured writer seems alive and well in the minds of many creatives.

But it doesn't *need* to be a tortured journey. It is uncomfortable at times, yes, but it is not a tortured journey.

You don't need a blueprint or a fast-action AI or a quick start to write your book in three days. You need to write.

The goal of this book is to help you get your first draft manuscript written.

You see, writing a book is a lot like parenting.

The first draft is your newborn—raw, alive, and full of potential. Getting it out of your mind, body, and soul is an act of creation in itself. This early stage is filled with wonder, love, and discovery. Everything is new. Each idea feels fresh and full of possibility. There are sleepless nights, and moments of pure magic, along with bursts of inspiration and unexpected frustrations. Just like those early years with a baby or toddler, you're often running on intuition and caffeine, but the joy keeps you going.

Then come the middle school years—your manuscript is awkward and uncertain, and so are you. You're experimenting with different voices and styles, trying things on like outfits in front of a mirror, and nothing seems to fit quite right. There are tantrums (yours), moments of self-doubt, and times you want to give up. But this is a necessary phase. Growth is happening, even if it's messy. Perseverance is everything.

As your manuscript matures, it enters the teenage phase. This is where things get both exhilarating and maddening. One day you're convinced you're writing something brilliant. The next, you think it's terrible. There's hope, bold new directions, and the ever-present doubt and self-sabotage. You see glimpses of what your book could be—what it wants to be—and sometimes, you even trust it.

And then, finally, with the help of wise editors (the coparents or mentors of this journey), your book becomes an adult. It's ready to step into the world. You've shaped it the best you could have. It's not perfect, but it's real, and it's yours. And just like with parenting, you learn that letting go is part of the process. You do all you can to get it ready for this world, but you can't plan for everything.

Writing a book is the same. You must have the long-haul view, the big picture. What will this book look like when it's completed? Whom will it help? Whom will it serve? What will bring you joy after publishing? What is your measure of success?

Envision your readers holding and responding to your book (with joy and excitement) and also imagine the other side of the coin, of not yet caring who you write to or your audience and readers.

You'll be thinking of the marketing and need not give it a second thought yet. Both are true. Set up your book launch but push it out of your mind for now.

Know that you will be tapping into your reader and understanding the purpose of your book, but for now, have the long-term view that you will eventually get it all done. For today, you'll just write.

Ready? Okay, let's do this.

Who? Me?

I ballroom dance. I've been dancing on and off my whole life. The point is: *on and off*. In spurts. I take off from it for many years at a time, and then I go back to it. I'm not very good, and yet I keep going. Why? It's frustrating and hard, and my feet have to twist at weird angles. It can hurt when I push my shoulders up and down or move my hips when I've been out of dance for months. I mostly like it, I think. I know that dance stretches me—more than just my body—and makes me grow.

But I am not a dancer, and not all my experiences have been positive. Many times, I've had reason to quit.

When I was seven, my mother enrolled me in a modern dance class. The instructor said I didn't have the physique for ballet, so I had to go into modern dance. Imagine: I was seven years old, and I was already labeled *unfit*. (I would later learn that adults tell children all the time what they can and cannot do, but I digress.)

After just three classes, I was politely asked to leave. My movements were thought to be tomboyish, ungraceful for even modern dance. My dance career was over.

Fast-forward to fourth grade. Our teacher thought it might be fun (?) to have us all learn the waltz. I was paired with a boy I barely knew, and we clumsily danced around in a box, barely hanging on one moment and grasping each other in case of death the next. "One-two-three, one-two-three" we counted as we stepped on each other. Awkward. We were both so embarrassed and mortified that I vowed never to dance again.

As a teenager, again, I was pushed into dance at school. Irish dance. Fast and complicated. After a single class, I fabricated injuries as my escape route and never went back. Then came the seventies and eighties—big hair bands and anything-goes moves on the dance floor. I swung my long hair back and forth and waved my arms wildly. I flourished on that dance floor. No rules, no expectations. Anything goes.

Good times.

Decades later, a whimsical decision led my husband and me to dabble in dance lessons. We found Brad, an award-winning competitive dance instructor. He instructed in swing, foxtrot, and samba. "Head up, keep your posture, and focus." "Look this way, that way, move your feet!"

We had a lot of fun, but we never really got the dancing routines down. Then, decades (yes, decades) passed when, a couple of years ago, I felt the urge to return to the dance floor. Why? Because it kept nagging at me. Something in me wanted to express itself in this way. Because dance should be fun, because I needed a creative outlet. Because, well, why not?

Reconnecting with Brad (thank you, Google!), I signed up for dance lessons spanning various styles, from foxtrot to cha-cha and my newfound favorite, West Coast swing. Week after week, I stumbled through the steps, forgetting whether to step forward or back, inside, or outside, and stepping on Brad. But I persisted. Tango, rumba, foxtrot—different dances, same mistakes.

Was I having fun yet?

I find learning dance quite frustrating. I know I must keep a beginner's mind, drop into my body, and allow it to be fun. I also know I mustn't take myself too seriously, and I will learn as I go. I am to pay attention and listen hard. I teach all of this and more about writing. We teach what we need to learn and learn what we need to teach, and when Brad speaks, I hear myself talking with my clients. We give the same advice. It's all the same when writing a book, building a business, or learning dance: Keep your head up, be in your body, and listen. Do your best. Have fun. Enjoy the process. Listen. Head up. Focus.

But was I having fun? *Not yet.*

Then, some time ago, Brad invited me to take part in a showcase event. Actually, it was a dance event with *judges*, but I didn't allow my mind to go down that dark hole.

I said no.

He asked again the next week, and I said no again.

When he asked the following week, I was worn down. Why not? I didn't have a good reason to say no, so I said yes.

I said yes mainly because I didn't know why I had said no. Was I scared? Insecure? Unsure? Those aren't reasons to say no, so I said yes.

I had a long inner talk with myself. I promised to enjoy the experience. I committed to focusing on learning and growth, not comparison or judgment. I told myself I would pretend to smile if needed (you know, the frozen smile that women learn to do when put on the spot). Overall, I resolved to have fun, watch other dancers, and cheer them on.

So, I did.

I danced eight dances, each with its share of missed steps and sometimes fake smiles. Cha-cha, foxtrot, nightclub two-step, rumba, East Coast swing, tango, waltz, and West Coast swing. Others danced, and I watched, waiting for my next turn, telling myself to breathe.

Ultimately, the judges were gentle; they clearly knew I was a beginner and gave me feedback fitting for a new dancer. It's never as bad as we make it in our heads. I got stickers, gold stars, and reviews to help me. Everyone clapped, and I clapped for others.

When it was over, my family asked if I had fun.

"Not really. It wasn't *fun*." Did I grow? *Yes*. Did I learn about myself? *Yes*. Do I know how to be a better dancer? *Absolutely!*

Would I do it again? *Yes!*

And now—much later—I remember it as fun. It wasn't fun in the moment, but now I see it as fun.

Writing your book is like dancing. Later, you'll remember it differently than how you experienced it. It will have been worth it.

Throughout this experience, I've deeply understood the parallels of "I am not a dancer," or "I am not a writer," or "I am not an author," or "I am not an entrepreneur."

What are we not... *yet*?

Now I say: "I am a dancer."

Writing a nonfiction book isn't just about putting words on a page—it's about capturing a message, sharing a purpose, and creating something that inspires others in a new and exciting way. Guiding authors through this process allows me to witness their growth, to help them overcome fears, and to ensure their unique voice reaches the people who need it most. Nonfiction writing is a bridge between experience and impact.

Who am I to dance? You may ask yourself: *Who am I to write?* Well, you have a message, a thought, an inkling. So, it's yours to write—not anyone else's. But what happens inside, when you work through your thoughts, will inspire you.

The most surprising thing I hear from our clients is about the personal transformation they experience while writing their book. This usually blindsides new authors. When writing, we must dig deep and figure out what we want to say and how to say it in a way that hasn't been said before. Our stories become very personal and intimate and oh-so transparent when put on paper. This isn't a casual conversation—our writing becomes permanent, and we are exposed. *We are out there.*

We have to choose where to put our stake in the sand, what we are going to say, and how we want to say it. We start asking ourselves: *Can I be bold, empathetic, or inspirational? What is the tone I want to set in the book? Where is my voice? Do I even have a voice? And is my voice distinct enough?*

When I was fifteen, we were given the homework assignment in English class to write a short story of our choosing. Being fifteen, I went into my experience, and a sappy love story was born! I'm old enough that all our homework at the time was handwritten. We didn't have typewriters at school and certainly no computers yet. So, I handwrote the story of two teenagers meeting at a café and instantly falling in love for ever after. It was good; I knew it was. It came from *my soul.* I was writing about what I knew and how I felt. During class, however, my English teacher held up my paper, clearly in my handwriting, with my name on the top, for everyone to see, stood up, and tore my short story in half.

He announced, "What drivel! You all can do better." And firmly instructed the class to write *real* literature.

As you can imagine, the shame of not being a "real" writer stuck with me. I couldn't write because I knew I'd be judged. My writing wasn't "real," and I wasn't good at it.

A side note: We don't come out of the womb knowing how to do stuff. That's a fallacy that bugs me. Parents, teachers, and bosses might say, "Why don't you know that? Did you ever learn that? Don't they teach that at school?"

Well, if we don't know it, we haven't learned it. That's not shameful.

We live a lifetime of learning, and we learn things when we learn them. We try, practice, try again, maybe get it, perhaps not. We might take a class or experiment, but we need a chance to learn, grow, and get it right and wrong.

You'll need to practice writing. Trying it. Finding your words. And, not sharing them before it's time.

As I got older, I wondered if my teacher realized those romance fiction authors whose books sell in airport kiosks are very successful and *real* writers—doing what they love, getting published, and making a living by being creative and following their hearts, even though it isn't "real" literature. Romance sells. And it's fun to write (so my romance authors tell me).

I realize now he was insensitive and might have been a tortured English teacher who wished he was writing and living his craft rather than teaching it. (This made-up story about his narrative makes me feel better anyway.)

As you can imagine, I didn't write fiction again. I'm not sure that I ever wrote again for that teacher; I can't remember. But I know I still haven't written any fiction—I haven't even tried.

It's not something I think about as a trauma anymore, he just sucked the joy out of writing fiction. Maybe I'll go back to it, maybe not. But I don't want this to happen to you. And life is funny. Here I am now, years later, running a publishing company, connecting and guiding authors and would-be writers. I do *not* teach the craft of writing, but I do encourage those who've been shut down, those who were told they weren't good enough, or those who, as teenagers, were told they couldn't write. If I can do it, you can do it. And you can do it differently—your way.

I used to tell myself, *I'm not a dancer.* Even though I loved to move, the word *dancer* felt too big, too official, too far from who I thought I was. Then, one day, I realized something: I dance. Not professionally, not even publicly, but I move, feel the rhythm, and connect to the music. That's enough. Dancing makes me a dancer.

The same is true for writing. You don't need a title, a publisher, or a polished manuscript to call yourself a writer. You need the courage to sit down and put your thoughts on paper. It's not about being perfect; it's about being in motion. It's about *doing the thing.*

So, how do you shift from "I'm not a writer" to "I am a writer"? It starts with the stories you tell yourself. Whenever you think *I'm not good enough,* replace it with, *I'm learning.* Every time you think, *This is terrible,* change it to, *This is the process.*

Writing is messy. It's creative, it's exploring. It's supposed to be a journey.

Your words don't need to be polished to have value. The act of writing itself is an accomplishment. Celebrate that. Each word you put on the page is a step forward, proof that you're showing up for yourself and your ideas. It counts whether you craft a sentence, paragraph, or page. You're doing the work. You're a writer.

The magic of writing comes from doing it. You don't become a writer by waiting for inspiration or by perfecting your craft in your head. You become a writer by writing. You have to show up for yourself. Even when it's hard, even when the words feel clumsy and the sentences don't flow, trust that the clarity and beauty will come. But first, you have to let yourself be a beginner and trust the process.

Being a first-time author isn't about publishing a bestseller or winning awards. It's about having the courage to express yourself, to put your ideas onto paper or a screen, even if it's *just* for you. It's about connecting to your purpose and trusting that your words matter. Putting your words out into the world is not to be considered until much later in the process.

So, next time you think, *I'm not a writer,* think about the words you've already written. Think about the stories, the ideas, the thoughts you've already put on paper. Those words make you a writer. You don't have to *earn* the title. You've already claimed it. Write like the writer you already are.

I'm Not Procrastinating, Am I?

Did you start yet? Great job if you did. As we know, getting started doesn't always mean you'll finish. Sometimes, you lose interest and motivation or get overwhelmed by fear or uncertainty.

Ask: Is what I'm procrastinating on important to my soul?

A lot of authors retire from a full career and then think they will write their book, but many never get to. One author I coached was a ninety-six-year-old man who shared with me the feeling that his soul would *wither away* if he didn't write his book! Dramatic? Maybe. However, he had dreamed of writing his book for thirty years! He'd had that desire since retiring from being a doctor at sixty years old. He came to me with a half-finished first draft, and together, we talked through his goals for the book and put together a writing schedule that would work for him. I gave him writing prompts based on an outline we created together. Finally, we went into editing and got his book published! He left a fabulous legacy for his family.

Another client, a woman in her eighties, pursued her dream of writing a book. After publishing, her life transformed, and she started speaking about her life all across her state—a surprise twist she never saw coming.

It's never too late.

Or too early. A seven-year-old recently wrote to me asking to publish his children's book. He sent his drawings, book outline, and a note about his dreams. I've also published several poetry books for teenagers. Age isn't a factor. If you have dreams, thoughts, goals, and hopes, you must act on those. Don't let age be your excuse. There are many legitimate reasons for not writing and publishing, and I'll cover some of those later; however, if you are putting it off, you might be in the procrastination trap.

We procrastinate for many reasons, but often, it boils down to a few key ones:

- We experience overwhelm which stops us in our tracks. We have to-do lists that are often impossibly long, filled with tasks that, honestly, don't matter. Most of our list could probably be ignored without consequence, but for some reason, we believe we cannot start writing until these things are complete.
- We chase every shiny new idea or distraction, thinking it's urgent or essential, or we think we can focus better if we spend some time doing the other thing first.
- We just don't know how to start. We may falsely believe the task is too difficult, or that we will do it wrong, or we are halted by the idea that there are so many ways to do it and that one could be the "right" way. Sometimes, we don't know where to begin.
- We worry too much about the end. How will I get this published? How many words or pages do I need? Should I go the print-on-demand route? How do I get into the library of congress? What if my mother, brother, and friends hate my book? We worry about the end so much that we don't even start.

Often, what's underneath all this is a kind of hesitation that stems from uncertainty—uncertainty about how to begin, how it will turn out, or whether it even matters. It may be the fear of being unable to set aside time to complete the task, *so why start at all?* We may have the fear of being unable to do it perfectly, so why not stop now—or never even start. It might even be fear of missing out on all the things that must be given up to then create the daily writing habits needed to see this thing through. So, why lose sleep, miss gatherings, disrupt a daily schedule, skip an annual vacation, or take paid time off to write instead of rest (and the list goes on).

And most of all, it's fear that you WILL do the thing. You'll write and publish, and no one will read it. Then you are faced with the thoughts, *I'm a failure.*

Failure says, "What if no one buys it?"

Success says, "What if everyone reads it and I'm suddenly visible?"

What if I clap my hands in the forest and no one hears? Does it matter? Yes. It matters. It matters to your soul.

Divine Timing Percolation

In my TEDx talk, I explore the concept that it's just not time yet. You aren't procrastinating. You are creating, thinking, wondering, exploring—percolating!

Think about the stories we've all heard about great works of art, music, or literature. Mozart didn't write his operas in a single sitting. *Don Giovanni* wasn't composed in a flurry of last-minute panic. It resulted from time, thought, and preparation—even if it looked like a burst of genius at the end.

When we procrastinate, we often think we're wasting time. But what if we're not wasting it at all? What if we're letting our ideas ripen? Sometimes, the most productive thing you can do is let something sit. If you are stuck, step away and trust that your subconscious is doing the work in the background.

We often treat procrastination like the villain in the story of productivity. We blame it for our missed deadlines, our unrealized dreams, and the nagging sense that we're not living up to our potential. But what if procrastination isn't always the enemy? What if it's simply the subconscious telling us it's not time yet? Sometimes, procrastination is just percolation.

When I wrote my first book, I spent years jotting down notes, tucking ideas into a file folder, and letting the concept simmer. I wasn't avoiding the work; I was letting the ideas grow. It wasn't until one day, when I found myself with a block of time, that everything clicked. I sat down, and in six weeks, the book was finished. But I couldn't have done that five years before that. I wasn't ready. It wasn't time yet.

There's a rhythm to creation, and it can't be forced. The waiting, the thinking, the quiet moments of reflection—all of that *is* part of the process. We get stuck when we confuse procrastination with readiness. You might tell yourself you are procrastinating, but maybe you're still gathering the pieces you need to move forward. Maybe you are not ready yet.

Of course, there's a fine line between percolation and distraction. It's one thing to let an idea stew in the back of your mind while you jot down notes and quietly prepare. It's another to scroll through social media for hours and call it "research." The difference is intention. Are you giving yourself the space to reflect or are you avoiding the task entirely?

When I'm in percolation mode, I write things down. I collect snippets of inspiration, ideas, and thoughts. Many of them are never explored further, they're simply written and recorded to make space for others to flow. I let them sit in a journal or a folder until they're ready to take shape.

Percolation is not about doing nothing; it's about allowing ideas to grow without forcing them. Think of it like this: You're preoccupied with thoughts of x, y, or z, and you find yourself circling back to them. You might even tell yourself, *Today I won't waste any more time ruminating on x. I've spent enough time planning for y. Z may never happen, so why do I keep thinking about it?*

Our brains are built to figure things out. They'll make things up if they don't have something real to work on. So, here's another way to look at it: If you take a minute to write it all down—the x, the y, the z—you free up mental space. It's like putting those thoughts in a parking lot to return to later. If they're important, you'll come back to them. If they're not, you've just allowed your brain to let them go.

On the flip side, rushing into action before you're ready can be just as unproductive. Have you ever started a project with half-formed ideas, only to end up scrapping it and starting over? It's like starting to plant your flower bed without proper preparation. Here's a gardening analogy: You've bought some amazing flowers, and you are super motivated to get them in the ground, but when you get to your bed, you realize it's overgrown with weeds, rabbits have dug holes in it, and ants have built mounds. You have a lot of work to do to get the bed ready for the planting if you expect the flowers to grow with any success. Sure, you can skip all the prep and hope for the best, but maybe you should wait. You can prep the bed, or your brain, by doing what's needed (weeding, filling in, relocating the ants, OR making notes, planning a schedule, meditating, and visualizing). When you give yourself the grace to wait, to percolate in writing, you're setting yourself up for a smoother process and a better result.

So, how do you know when it's time to move from percolation to action? It's a feeling, a readiness that can't be forced. For me, it has been like flipping a switch. One day, the ideas that have been simmering suddenly come together, and I know it's time to act. It's not about waiting forever; it's about waiting for the right moment.

If you've been beating yourself up for procrastinating, maybe it's time to reframe it or at least look at it through a different lens. Ask yourself: Is this procrastination, or is this percolation? Am I avoiding the work, or am I letting the work come to me? There's a big difference.

Percolation is about waiting for the right time, while procrastination comes from distractions or avoidance. There's a clear difference between preparing and getting distracted.

When I thought about my writing for a long time, I collected notes, jotted down ideas, and kept them in a folder. Then one day, it was time, and I sat down to write. It wasn't procrastination; it was percolation. Sometimes, it takes time for things to be ready.

The truth is, not everything can be rushed. Some things take time. Trust the process. Let your ideas brew. And when the time is right, take that first step. You'll know when you're ready.

Deadlines can be powerful motivators. Many of us work better with them. They can provide structure and a sense of urgency. For example, the author in his nineties who had always dreamed of writing a book knew it was now or never. Sometimes, it's as simple as that—a clear, unavoidable deadline that forces action. And the flip of that is sometimes deadlines cause more stress and can even force a person to shut down based on how they are wired. Know how you operate, understand yourself, your heart, your wisdom. Learn how you best make decisions, move forward, and respond to deadlines. Some people work well under pressure; others crack.

None of this is one-size-fits-all. That's why blueprints and systems don't always work. We are not wired the same and we are all inspired and guided in different ways with different motivators.

Procrastination isn't inherently bad. It's information. It tells us where we're stuck, what we're afraid of, or what doesn't align with our purpose. Instead of shaming yourself for procrastinating, ask: What is this telling me? Am I avoiding this task because it doesn't matter or because I'm afraid to fail? Use that information to move forward.

Procrastination in writing comes from fear or self-doubt, often stemming from not feeling ready or clear about what you want to say. If you don't get started, it may be because you're not sure of your message. Begin by getting over yourself; start writing with a beginner's mind. You don't have to be perfect; you just need to get it out of your head. The good news is, if you're procrastinating, it might mean you just need clarity. Maybe you need to refine your purpose or figure out how to express it. Once you find your way through self-doubt, you'll get started.

So, the next time you find yourself procrastinating, take a moment. Appreciate the space it's creating. Use it to reflect, prioritize, and prepare. And when the time is right, move. Take the first step, even if it's small. The world needs your ideas, your creativity, and your action. Stop waiting. Start doing. Trust in Divine timing.

No one is meant to do it all alone. Select a buddy or buddies who you can turn to when you are having a hard time finding the way—a friend, a coach, or a prayer partner. Get the help you need. Ask for support. Let someone hold your hand and walk you through the steps. It's not weakness; it's wisdom.

There is another trap for many writers: perfectionism. You believe you need it to be flawless, but no book ever is. Knowing that every author faces this, you must overcome the fear of criticism and rejection. Overcoming this fear is about trusting the process and allowing yourself to create without judgment. Fear is often overcome by preparation, because when you feel prepared, you're more confident, making fear easier to handle. Start with a draft, knowing it can always be improved later. Include everything and know it can be rearranged or cut down later. It's called a first draft for a reason, because we expect to go into rewrites. Don't judge. Trust the process. Allow your thoughts to spill out onto the page, knowing there will be many opportunities.

Fear or Unknowing?

Fear is a powerful force. It's often the whisper in the back of your mind telling you that you're not ready, don't know enough, or might fail. But here's the truth: Fear isn't always rooted in reality. More often than not, it results from a gap in information. I'm not talking about facing a bear in the wilderness—I'm talking about the fear that stops us from living to our fullest potential. Think about the last time you felt paralyzed by fear. Maybe you were starting a new project, launching a business, or even writing a book. Did your fear stem from a real threat, or was it the uncertainty of not knowing what steps to take next? When we don't have enough information, our brains fill in the gaps—and often, they fill them with worst-case scenarios.

The antidote to fear is knowledge and preparation. Preparation means seeking out the information you need to feel confident and qualified. It's about learning what you don't know and transforming uncertainty into clarity. Fear thrives in the unknown, but when you illuminate those dark corners with knowledge, its power diminishes.

This doesn't mean you need to know everything. Waiting until you feel 100 percent ready might mean waiting forever. Instead, focus on what you need to know to take the next step. Gather just enough information to move forward, and let each small step build your confidence. You'll get more clarity as you go.

Fear can also be a sign that you're about to do something meaningful. It's often the companion of growth and change, nudging you toward something bigger than yourself. Instead of letting fear stop you, let it guide you. Ask: What do I need to learn? What tools, resources, or support will help me take the next step? Is this important to me? Am I afraid I might fail?

Remember, fear isn't your enemy. It's a messenger. It shows you where you need more clarity, more preparation, or maybe just a little more courage. When you embrace it, fear becomes a catalyst for growth.

If you're staring at a blank page, remember, you've already got knowledge. Now it's time to put it in one place. You can sort it out later, maybe alone, but likely with a coach or an editor.

Use your resources. Tap it out. Talk it out. Get a coach. Walk. Sing. Scream. Whatever works. But get the knowledge out of your head and onto the page.

Play mind games if you have to: I'm a writer, an author, a teacher. I have a mission right now: to complete this book. I'm not at the whim of my unconscious to sabotage myself. Although I may not be the best, fastest, or most accomplished writer, I am writing. And I keep writing.

You are not waiting for the muse to strike. We hope it does, and when it happens, it's joyful and magical. But for that flow to show up, you have to begin—with pen to paper, with an open heart and a mind full of self-love. You have to allow the process to begin.

Most first-time writers need to mind-dump. Get it all out—all the stories, thoughts, ideas. Don't worry about what will or won't end up in the final book. Don't censor yourself in the first draft. Let it rip.

Later, you'll decide what stays. But if you try to filter and perfect everything in the beginning, you'll stall out. That kind of pressure kills creativity.

I love my computer. I can type fast. I learned from my mom, who could type 120 words per minute and typed out menus with carbon paper every night at our restaurant. Typing is fast and freeing for me.

Writing by hand is slower, but magical. It links the brain, heart, and body in a different way. The ideas flow through your arm and onto the page. Try it. Write in a journal for fifteen minutes. Dump it all out—your day, your thoughts, your to-do list. Then, when your mind is clearer, open your laptop and write another thirty minutes. That's your book time.

If the fear is loud, it just means the book matters. So write anyway.

Writer's Block

When you hit a wall, and you will, that doesn't mean you're not a writer. It means you're in the thick of it. It's that feeling when you sit down to write, but the words just won't come. You stare at the blank page, and your mind lacks ideas. You start to wonder if you're cut out for this writing thing after all. Maybe you clean your silverware drawer, or do laundry, or call about the insurance bill sitting on your desk. Anything but write. Anything but face failure as a writer.

Don't force brilliance. Having an expectation that you'll sit down and crank out 500 or 5,000 usable words is the fastest way to freeze. Some days the words flow; other days, you just show up.

If you're stuck, try writing a letter instead of a chapter. Outline bullet points instead of whole paragraphs. Freewrite garbage to get moving. It all counts. The point is to stay in motion.

One trick I teach is to set your manuscript aside for a day, a week, or whatever feels right. Use that time to create—paint rocks, walk, cook, wander a thrift shop. Take yourself on a solo artist date (thank you, Julia Cameron). Give your brain space, and trust that's still part of the writing.

If you're on deadline, take short breaks—move your body, make a snack, scream, dance, sing—then return and write anything. It's about momentum, not perfection.

Writing prompts can also help. Use a random word, a question, a memory. Let it unlock something. Freewriting bypasses the inner critic and wakes up your creative mind. Give yourself a scenario, a question, or even a single word, and write a short passage based on that prompt. These creative bursts can help you unlock new ideas and get words flowing. You can create your own or search the internet for a list that will help you tap into that process.

Don't worry, maybe your brain is in percolation. Perhaps you don't have anything to say today. Maybe your creative juices need a jump start, and perhaps you just need a writing prompt to get you going.

It's okay to pause and let your mind meander. That quiet space is where insight often shows up. You don't have to be a tortured soul getting up at 3:00 a.m. or writing through the night. You just need to write and when you can't, do something fun. Let go, stop pushing. Take a break and then come back to your writing renewed and with new eyes.

Remember that writer's block is natural and happens to everyone at some point, even the most successful writers! Don't beat yourself up over it; instead, focus on finding techniques that work for you personally.

Overcoming writer's block during the first draft stage requires patience, perseverance, and flexibility. By taking breaks when needed, trying new techniques like freewriting and brainstorming, and being open-minded about changing your approach and process can help keep it fresh. Another tip is collaboration. Be willing to bounce ideas off friends or other writers in online communities or workshops. Sometimes talking through ideas with others can spark new perspectives and fresh ideas.

Walking Into Creativity

Years ago, I had the privilege of attending a writing retreat in Taos with Natalie Goldberg, the author of *Writing Down the Bones*. It was an experience that reshaped the way I approach writing, creativity, and even the act of living. One of the most profound exercises we did was something so simple, yet so transformative: walking.

We walked. Not briskly, not with a destination in mind, but slowly and mindfully. It wasn't about exercise or getting anywhere. It was about the act of walking itself. Step by step, we moved through the beautiful landscapes of Taos, letting our feet touch the earth, our breath find its rhythm, and our minds quiet down.

The process of slow, mindful walking has a way of clearing out the mental clutter. As we walked, the noise in our heads began to settle. The endless to-do lists, the doubts, the fears—all of it seemed to fade with each step. Walking grounded us in our bodies, reconnecting us to the present moment. And in that quiet, grounded space, something incredible happened: Our creativity opened up.

When we returned to our notebooks, the writing flowed. Ideas that had been stuck or elusive suddenly came to life. The act of walking had created space in our minds, in our bodies, and on the page. It wasn't magic; it was movement—the simple act of walking that cleared space for creativity. A deliberate, mindful movement that brought us back to ourselves and to the creative wellspring within.

This practice stayed with me long after the retreat. Whenever I feel stuck or overwhelmed, I remember those walks in Taos. I put on my shoes, step outside, and let the act of walking do its work. It's a reminder that creativity doesn't always come from sitting and forcing the words. Sometimes, it comes from moving, from breathing, from simply being.

Natalie Goldberg taught us that writing isn't just a mental exercise; it's a full-body experience. And in Taos, through the simple act of walking, I learned to trust the process, to let go of the noise, and to make space for the words to come. Sometimes, the best way to get unstuck is to take a step. Then another. And another.

Writing What's Right in Front of You

At the same retreat in Taos with Natalie Goldberg, we didn't just write—we paid attention. We listened, we watched, we observed. We paid attention to the details and wrote about whatever was in front of us: a pen, the paper, a tree outside the window, the teacup in our hands, or the person sitting across the room. We wrote about the chair we were sitting on, not just its appearance, but how it felt beneath us, how the wood smelled faintly of polish or years of use. We learned to pay attention.

This practice was more than just putting words on a page. It was about noticing. Really noticing. We were encouraged to use all of our senses—to describe how things felt, smelled, looked, sounded, even tasted. The goal wasn't to create a masterpiece but to connect deeply with the moment and let the writing emerge from that connection.

I remember staring at a tree outside the window. Just a tree, until I really watched it. The bark, rough and weathered, the branches twisting against the endless blue of the Taos sky. The air was dry, with a hint of sagebrush carried on the breeze. My pen moved across the page, capturing not just the tree but how it felt to be there, in that room, in that moment. I wasn't just writing about the tree; I was writing *my experience* of the tree and how its strength made me feel grounded, how its roots reminded me to stay present.

Another time, I wrote about the teacup in my hand. The rim was chipped, the handle smooth from years of being held. The tea inside was still warm, its steam curling upward and carrying the faint aroma of chamomile. I wrote about how the cup felt against my fingers, how the tea tasted slightly earthy and sweet. It wasn't really about the teacup. It simply brought me into the moment and helped me notice what I was feeling.

Even something as ordinary as the chair beneath me became extraordinary through writing. The wood pressed firm against my back, the cushion worn thin in places. I noticed how my legs rested against the edge, how the chair creaked slightly when I shifted my weight. Writing about the chair wasn't just about the chair, it was about grounding myself in my senses and letting the words flow from there.

This exercise taught me that writing isn't about inventing something out of thin air. It's about paying attention to what's already there. By focusing on the details, the sights, sounds, smells, and textures—we open ourselves up to deeper creativity. The words come naturally when we let ourselves truly see and feel the world around us.

In Taos, I learned that writing isn't about big ideas or profound insights. It's about noticing the small things, the everyday moments, and giving them the attention they deserve. When we do that, the ordinary becomes extraordinary and the page fills with life. And it all starts by looking at what's right in front of you.

Purpose, Mission, and Message

Now, before you start writing:

Wait, what? I've spent all this time encouraging you to just write, start writing, get words on paper, just write! But first, I want you to think about the book, the readers, the audience, and your message. So, before you write the book, I will ask you to think about a few things.

Your purpose!

Are you a teacher, healer, or storyteller? A philosopher, scientist, therapist, or coach? Do you have a different way of explaining something? Have you stumbled upon a synthesis of information that might make something easier for humanity? Have your experiences cultivated a unique view that you feel particularly moved to share? You have a unique mission or message. You might want to read that again. *You* have a *unique* mission or message. No matter where you are in the process, if you are just beginning or nearly there, you know this book holds a greater purpose. Now is the time to bring it forward. The greater your connection with your purpose, the easier it will be to continue when the writing gets hard or when you can't find the words or have moments of self-doubt. Tap back into your purpose and remind yourself:

- I'm here to share.
- I have wisdom.
- I'm a teacher.
- I am a natural storyteller.

- I have an important message for…

Whatever it is for you, keep in touch with that feeling.

Purpose is fundamentally about being rather than doing. It's not just about what you achieve but how you exist in alignment with your truth. Your writing and book will push you to get even more aligned with your truth, inspiring you to live your purpose fully. Writing a book forces you to stay true to who you are, what you want to say, and how you want to say it. Even if you are the only person who reads it (for now), you'll be more confident in who you are, you will grow and be more rooted in purpose.

Once you're grounded in your purpose and connected to your core energy, you can clearly focus on the message and direction of your book. You'll feel proud of the book itself and who you've become in the process.

When you are grounded in purpose, outlining, writing, and publishing become natural steps that are an extension of purpose.

Your *mission* is the broader, underlying purpose or goal that drives you to write the book in the first place. It's what you hope to achieve not only for yourself but also for your readers. It's about what you want to contribute to the world, field, or community. A mission might stem from your experiences, ability, or passion for a subject. It shapes the book's essence— whether it's to inspire, educate, challenge, or entertain.

Your mission may also help answer the question: *Why am I writing this book?* It's the long-term vision of what the book is meant to accomplish and how it connects to a larger purpose in your life as the writer.

On the other hand, the *message* is the specific point or set of ideas that you are communicating through the book. It's the content, insights, or lessons that you want your readers to take away. Your message is the actual information or per-spective that will resonate with those who read your work. It's what you're trying to say and share with the world, in a way that leaves an impact on the audience.

Your message may answer the question: What do I want my readers to know, feel, or do as a result of reading my book? It's the core of the book.

Once connected to your purpose (teaching, inspiring, shar-ing, healing), you will be able to connect your mission (e.g., to share my teaching with a million people), and your mes-sage (e.g., that you can eat potatoes and lose weight—more on that later) with the people who are ready to hear it.

First, what is your purpose? Choose from these verbs or add your own.

- Teaching
- Healing
- Inspiring
- Creating
- Networking
- Guiding
- Leading
- Transforming
- Connecting
- Empowering
- Mentoring
- Building
- Sharing
- Envisioning
- Nurturing
- Awakening
- Elevating
- Supporting
- Embodying
- Activating
- Expanding
- Manifesting
- Uplifting
- Cultivating
- Channeling

Then once you ground into your verb, ask how your book helps you move your purpose forward. What is your mission? For example, is it to reach more people, to leave a legacy, to heal people's trauma, or to help children eat better?

And what message are you sharing? *That's* the premise of your book.

Your Premise

You've got to choose one main point.

It's okay to have a ton of ideas floating around. We all do. I've got lots of ideas and lots of interests, but I'm not putting all my ideas and interests into one book. You need to start with one clear takeaway. You may need to write down all the ideas. Pick the one idea that feels most urgent, the one you can't stop thinking about. You may need to write down all your ideas. Get them out of your head and onto paper, giving them space to breathe, clearing the way for other thoughts. Rest your brain, knowing you don't need to write a book out of every single one of these ideas. You'll choose and pick your top one or two ideas and see if they align with the purpose and mission and then the message you want to share.

If your purpose is rooted in inspiration, maybe you'll write a book emphasizing that (i.e., if I can do it, so can you). You'll understand your purpose, then lean into your messaging, which might be that others can rise up and do hard things. Then, write the book based on that.

Or say for example, if you are an introverted salesperson, you might write a book about how to easily connect with others in an isolated society, how introversion can be a friend, and how networking one-on-one (instead of in big groups) is the best route for growing certain people's productivity. Then, you might teach sales in a unique way through your book.

Your purpose comes first, then the mission, then your premise, then the messaging through the book.

Your Readers!

Now, you've got some words on paper napkins, note cards, your computer, and your phone. It's time for the next step.

Find out who wants and needs your book and your message and keep them in mind as you write. Write to them.

If you aren't sure where to start with this, I have a meditation online that you can find on the resources page. This will take you through a short, guided visualization/meditation to help you find and connect with your readers.

First, the questions:

- What is your personal purpose?
- What is your core message?
- Who needs your book?
- How do you align your message with your book?
- What is the purpose of your book, and who is it truly for?
- Who wants to read your book?

Often, we think, *Everyone needs to hear my message*. But that's not true. Not everyone cares. You may know they *need* it, but if they don't *want* it, your book will never reach them. Loads of people want to lose weight, some even need to lose weight, but if you have a weight loss book, you better stand out from the crowd. Do you have an inspiring personal story? A unique method, science behind your words?

Who do you think you will most help? Women over fifty? That's a different book than a book for a young man.

Does your book speak to a USA audience or an international audience? Health-conscious eaters or runners?

- Who will be reading your book? Who is the avatar of that person? Do they all shop at a dollar store or a high-end organic store? Do they camp or prefer all-inclusive resorts? Are they nature lovers or art enthusiasts? Flesh this out. Be as descriptive as possible. *See* your readers in your mind's eye. Connect with them. Tear out photos from magazines that represent your reader. Understand them from the inside out.

Write to your people, the ones who need and want what you have.

Better to be a big fish in a small pond than a small fish in a big pond. You've got to stand out for your community of readers.

Before diving into audience research, take a moment to reflect on the transformation you want to offer your reader.

Ask yourself: Who am I writing for? What change will they experience because of my book? How does my personal story or expertise connect with their struggles or desires?

Your core message lives at the intersection of your purpose, your story, and your readers' needs. To uncover it, work through these questions:

- What do you want your reader to know, learn, or do after reading your book?
- What is the biggest takeaway?

For instance, I hope that after reading *this* book, you'll be inspired to act on your own. You'll know you are worthy, ready, and have a few tools to help you get started.

Now, begin creating your reader avatar—a detailed profile of your ideal reader. Consider the following:

- **Demographics:** age, gender, location, education level, profession
- **Psychographics:** values, interests, goals, and challenges
- **Behavior:** where they spend time online, what books they read, how they consume content, and who they trust. Do they go to church? Hike? Travel? Do they share your values or life experiences? Get as detailed as you can.

Go deeper:

- Who can you best serve?
- What emotional connection drives your audience?
- What problems can you solve for them?
- Who are your current clients or followers? What wisdom do they say they gain from you?
- Who were you a few years ago? Decades ago? What do you wish someone had told you when you needed it most?
- Think about what will draw your readers in and what they will gain by reading your words. Readers are drawn to books that solve a problem or fulfill a desire. Identify the following to help get you pointed in a direction:
- The pain point: What challenge does your book address?
- The results: What outcomes can readers expect?
- The process: What steps or inspiration will you provide?

Imagine a room filled with your readers. What do they have in common? What are their struggles and goals? Craft your book to meet them where they are.

You might even consider creating a vision board of these future readers. Choose one potential reader and mentally ask them what they love about your book or what experience they want to have with your writing. (This can be a helpful writing exercise, too!) Have fun with this! It's exciting to imagine the impact your words will have on them.

Your reader needs something. Maybe they want to feel better in their body, and you *know* yoga can help, but you think yoga has gotten a bad rep with the contortions on the fronts of magazines. Y*ou know* yoga is about being present in the body that a person has, not about changing it into some pretzel. The key is finding where your knowledge intersects with their needs.

If you don't know exactly who your audience is, you risk missing the people your message is meant to reach. Is your reader someone who already loves yoga or someone new to it? Your marketing and messaging will shift based on who you're connecting with.

Start with yourself: Are you writing for an audience who is where you were a few years or decades ago? Do you wish you had had this book before you started a specific project? Are you writing to inspire a younger you? Are you writing the book for a different (or even future) version of yourself? This is your mission and purpose, and your book must stay aligned with your passion. Only then can you successfully reach the right audience with a message that connects deeply with them.

Years ago, I had a client, Beth, who was just beginning in her field. She had an idea to write a book about her unique take on healing the body. At the time, her work was groundbreaking, paving the way for the mind-body connection in healing. Today, she's a respected voice in her field, with a thriving business built around her book.

When we started working together, she had many ideas from her small practice, but she needed help finding her unique niche, voice, and plan for connecting her ideas with her future readers. We went through the same steps I'm taking with you now.

A decade after her book was published, Beth consistently sells books, brings people into her online community (through her book link), signs up new practitioners, and hears from those who have healed their pain. She would call herself a successful author, although you've probably never heard of her. In her niche, she's a rock star.

I want the same for you.

Let's say you're writing a book about yoga. You have a unique take on it, and you want to show how yoga is accessible to everyone, anywhere. You might think your book is for everybody. But the truth is, not everyone cares. After all, some people are tired of hearing about all its benefits and applications. It seems to be a catch-all in some circles.

How do you connect with the people who *do* care? How do you find those who will read and benefit from your book now?

If your reader wants to feel better in their body, they may not have explored yoga yet. If you market exclusively using the term *yoga*, you might miss a significant portion of your audience. Alternatively, if your reader is immersed in yoga, you'll want your marketing to reflect that expertise.

This begins with your mission and your purpose. Your book has been inspired by you, and your passion will keep you aligned as you connect with your audience.

These steps will help you define your message, audience, and the book that connects deeply with your readers.

After you've figured out and envisioned your reader, you'll want to do some market research. What is already out there? What is missing in the marketplace? Why and how are you and your ideas unique to this audience?

Research Similar Books

Look at books similar to yours or similar to what you hope yours will look like upon completion. Check online reviews and notice what readers liked and what they didn't. Pay attention to how reviewers describe themselves and their needs. These are your potential readers too.

Analyze Social Media Conversations

Search hashtags, groups, or forums where people discuss topics related to your book. This will help you understand the language they use and the issues they care about. You can get as involved as you like to understand the nuance of future readers better.

Survey Potential Readers

Create a short survey and share it with your network or online communities. Ask questions about their interests, challenges, and what they look for in books on your topic. Listen carefully!

Identify the Problems or Desires

Make a list of the specific problems, questions, or desires your book aims to address and how yours will fill some of the gaps you have found in your research. How is yours different? For example, if you're writing a business book, think about what challenges your book will help readers solve—starting a business, improving leadership skills, or growing sales, and highlight the ways this information is missing in the books already out there, or how yours will build upon or enhance those that are widely read.

Seeing your reader, hearing their concerns and questions, and knowing you have the answers will help you stay focused on the message you are sending through the creation of your book. Remember, the world needs to hear you and read your words.

The Tools You Need

You don't need the perfect space, the right pen, or any special tools to start writing. It's nice when the setup feels just right—but it's not required.

I used to think I needed a cabin by a lake to really write. Now I write in my kitchen, my office, even in hotel rooms. Writing is like that. You use what you have, and you begin.

Think about Maya Angelou. She's one of the most iconic writers of our time, and she wrote some of her best work in less-than-ideal conditions. Picture her sitting up in the middle of the night, a baby feeding, spit-up on her shoulder, scribbling words that would change the world. She didn't wait for the right moment or the right tools. She wrote because she had something to say, and she used whatever scraps of time and energy she could find.

If Maya Angelou could write through the exhaustion of motherhood in the middle of the night, what's stopping you? We let the idea of "the perfect setup" hold us back. We tell ourselves we need a dedicated space, a special pen, or a ritual to start. But here's the truth: Writing is about the commitment, not the environment.

But I've learned that we do not need a special writing space. It's nice but not necessary.

My dad, a professional chef (as well as an entrepreneur and an all-around accomplished great guy), cooked anywhere and everywhere: in his fabulous professional kitchen, at my tiny apartment when I first moved out, in friends' kitchens, on a barbecue, or on a camp cookstove.

He didn't need his fancy pots and knife set or fancy ingredients. He had them and enjoyed them when they were available, but he never relied on them.

He just cooked.

Writing is like that.

You might have a favorite space or setup, but when it's time to write, none of that matters. What matters is showing up.

Stephen King has a dedicated writing space, and he shows up to his shed behind his home every morning to write. He sits down to write, and he writes.

In his book *On Writing*, Stephen King writes, "Amateurs sit and wait for inspiration. The rest of us just get up and go to work."

It's that simple. Don't let your space or lack of inspiration stop you. Just write. Anything. Write.

You will get better; it will get easier. You may only ever write one book, or you may write more. It doesn't matter today. Today, what matters is that you write.

Your writing doesn't care if you're sitting at a desk or on the floor, if you're typing on a laptop or jotting notes on the back of an old receipt. The words don't care if you're rested, organized, or even coherent. They just want to come out. And if you're waiting for everything to be perfect, you're going to be waiting a long time.

Inspiration and writing happen in the moments of life. Maybe it's five minutes while the coffee brews or a quick note typed on your phone during a meeting. Maybe it's late at night when the house is quiet, or early in the morning before the chaos of the day begins. You don't need hours; you just need minutes to start.

Grab whatever's nearby and start. A napkin, an envelope, your phone. It doesn't matter. What matters is getting the words out of your head and onto something tangible. You can always clean it up later. For now, capture it.

Stop waiting for inspiration, for time, for quiet, for the perfect conditions. Writing isn't about waiting; it's about doing. Maya Angelou didn't wait, and neither should you. Write through the spit-up, the noise, the chaos. Write because you have something to say. The world needs your words, and it won't wait for you to find the perfect pen.

What tools do you really need? Just a willingness to show up, the right mindset, and permission to write messy first drafts. The willingness, mindset, and availability allow you to write crap and know you won't screw it up.

Get words on paper. Write. Now.

Section II
Time to Get to Writing

Hacks

If you're just starting to write for the first time, it can feel over-whelming. The blank page! That blank page has a way of staring back at you, daring you to make the first move.

Here's the truth: You don't need to have it all figured out. You just need to start. And sometimes, starting means using a little trick or a shortcut to push past the resistance and get your first words down.

The tools and hacks below are to help you get the first words down. They're about getting unstuck. They're about helping you move from "I want to write" to "I'm writing." That's the only step that matters right now.

Writing Prompts

Create your own writing prompts! What do you want to write about? What needs to go into your book? Make a short list of ideas, thoughts, words that you'll write about at some point.

My list for this book might look like this:

- Procrastination
- Percolation
- What is the Purpose of the book?
- Why write?
- Who should write?
- Editors
- Publishing

- Fear
- My TEDx talk

And on and on. When I am not inspired, I'll look at my list and write for ten minutes on one of the topics. It doesn't need to be in any correct order, just thoughts to write about. You can come up with all sorts of writing prompts, and mine are just a few examples. You'll find tons online if you search for writing prompts to get you going.

Sometimes, I can't figure out how to start—even when I know what I want to say. The idea is in my head, but the words won't come. Writing helps me work through the tangle and find clarity. That's when I write whatever's right in front of me: the coffee, the photo of my daughter, my puppy on her bed. I write about that for five or ten minutes, training my muse to show up on cue—not waiting for inspiration to strike (paraphrased from Stephen King's *On Writing*).

Speech to Text

Wait, do I have to *write?* Maybe you believe you are a better speaker than a writer. Or you have a lot more experience with your voice than your pen. You teach, speak, tell stories, coach, or spend a lot of time talking and want to text your notes to yourself. That works (somewhat). I often speak into my phone. Notes, thoughts, ideas, and complete paragraphs can come out in surprising clarity. However, once they are transcribed and I look at them on paper, they still need a lot of work. Rarely is a sentence ready to use from transcribed audio. We speak in a more casual, scattered way with *ums* and *ahs* and incomplete sentences. Don't be discouraged if your transcribed words need work. That's normal. And transcription is a tool. So, use it to get your ideas flowing—and keep going. Say what's on your mind. Then read it back and smooth it into something that makes sense on the page.

Your Back Cover (The Synopsis)

When I work with authors, I ask them to write a draft of their back cover copy early in the process. Not because it will stay the same—it usually changes before publishing—but because it gives clarity and direction. It's a way to anchor your writing.

Begin with clarity on the outcome. What should your reader feel, know, or do by the end? Look at books in your genre— pull some off your own shelf or browse a bookstore. Read the back covers and notice what works. This draft synopsis becomes your North Star. It keeps you focused as you write and helps you stay aligned with your core message.

And remember: the back cover speaks to your reader. It's less about what's in the book and more about what the reader will take away. It should make them *want* to read it. And it should remind you why your message matters and why you're the one to share it.

Your Last Chapter

Another useful tip: Write your last chapter first.

This isn't about rushing to the end—it's about getting clear. The last chapter is where everything you've written comes together. It's where your main message lands. Writing it early on helps you focus your ideas and stay on track as you move through the rest of the book.

Think of it as setting your destination before the journey.

Outline

We all have different learning and organizational styles. The question is: How do *you* work best?

Some writers thrive with a clear outline from the start—it helps break the book into manageable pieces and keeps the structure flowing logically from chapter to chapter. A good outline acts like a roadmap. It can help you avoid overwhelm and stay focused on the big picture without losing track of the details.

I've worked with first-time authors who could "see" their book as a table of contents. Just by naming the chapters early, they were able to sort through their ideas, stay organized, and ensure they didn't forget any important insights along the way. These chapter titles gave them structure, small goals to aim for, and helped keep the tone and message consistent throughout.

Here's one way to approach it:

Take your core message and break it into three main points. Then, break each of those points down again.

Just for fun, here's a ridiculous example:

Let's say your reader is a woman over fifty who has tried every diet. And let's say your core message is: *Eat potatoes, lose weight!* (Totally not true—just an absurd example.)

From there, you'd break that message into parts:

- Why everything else hasn't worked
- The science of the potato plan
- How to love your new body, one spud at a time

Even this silly example shows how this structure can help shape your content—and keep your reader engaged.

Let's keep going with the potato book example.

Core Message: *Eat potatoes, lose weight!*

It's a wild (and totally fictional) premise—but it works to illustrate how to break down your book's structure.

Start with three main ideas:

1. Find potatoes you love.

2. Try new types of potatoes.

3. Experiment with cooking styles.

Now break those ideas down further:

Potatoes I love:

- Russets
- Goldens
- Idaho

New types of potatoes to try:

- Red Potato – Waxy and firm; great for salads and roasting
- Fingerling Potato – Small and knobby; perfect roasted
- Purple Potato – Vibrant and earthy; great boiled or roasted
- White Potato – Thin skin, creamy inside; ideal for frying and mashing
- Sweet Potato – Naturally sweet; great baked or in casseroles
- Petite Potato – Tiny and tender; roast whole
- New Potato – Young, early-harvested; best for boiling or salads
- Adirondack Blue – Blue skin and flesh; mild flavor, great baked or boiled

Ways to cook potatoes:

- Baked – Fluffy inside, crispy outside
- Mashed – Classic comfort
- Roasted – Golden and crisp
- Fried – Chips, fries, you name it
- Boiled – Simple and perfect for salads
- Grilled – Smoky, charred flavor

- Scalloped – Creamy, cheesy layers
- Steamed – Light, soft, healthy
- Sautéed – Crispy cubes with herbs
- Hash Browns – Shredded and fried to perfection

And just like that, you've got the bones of a book. Add in real stories, and now it's a fun, engaging, and unexpectedly impactful potato book.

You may need to start by dumping all your ideas out first. Just get them down. Then go back and look at your main takeaways. What do you want your reader to walk away with—and start organizing from there. You might find that your scattered thoughts naturally fall into sections or even full chapters.

Whether you're outlining, brainstorming, or just scribbling ideas, the goal is clarity. Clarity for you as the writer and for your reader as they follow along. The kind of book you're writing—whether it's a memoir, how-to, or big idea book—will help shape the structure. Take time to plan your chapters in a way that reflects your message and speaks to your audience.

Potatoes optional.

Write Now, Edit Later

Everything you write in the beginning is fluid. It's not set in stone, and it's definitely not supposed to be perfect. At this stage, you're just getting your thoughts down. Think of your first draft more like journaling—unfiltered, messy, and honest. That's exactly how it should be.

You're not writing a polished book right now. You're making space. You're clearing the noise so the good stuff can show up.

Julia Cameron calls this practice *Morning Pages*. It's about writing by hand, first thing in the morning, without editing or judgment. It's a brain dump. You write down whatever's swirling around in your head—even if it's half-formed thoughts, random to-dos, or that one story about Uncle Jim you'd never actually include in your book.

The point isn't to get it "right." The point is to be real.

When you build this habit, you'll start to notice more clarity. You'll go deeper in your writing. And when it's time to sit down and work on your book, the page won't feel quite so intimidating.

Writing is like digging through layers of dirt to get to the treasure buried underneath. The first layers might be messy, but they're necessary. If you spend all your energy looking at the dirt, you'll never get to the gold.

So don't worry about the writing yet. Don't stress over whether it's good or bad. Just write. Let the words tumble out, imperfect and chaotic. Write as if no one is ever going to read it. Write as if it doesn't matter—because at this moment, it doesn't. What matters is that you're writing.

Later, you can decide what stays and what goes. You can turn the messy bits into magic and make sure Uncle Jim doesn't look too bad in the final draft (if you want). But for now, let it all out. The only way to get to the good stuff is to move through the rest.

Trust the process. Write now, edit later.

Types of Books

Structure

When you start writing, one of the first things to consider is the type of book you're creating. Are you envisioning a workbook filled with exercises and prompts to guide your readers step by step? Or perhaps it's a memoir, sharing your journey in a way that connects deeply with others? Maybe you're leaning toward a business book to establish yourself as an expert and share strategies that help others succeed. A how-to book could be your way of offering practical advice to solve a problem or teach a skill. Self-help books may provide actionable steps to greater freedom and ease in life. Whatever type of book you're writing, it's essential to understand its purpose and the audience you're speaking to. This clarity will shape everything from your tone to the way you structure your chapters. Consider each.

A workbook is interactive, guiding the reader through exercises, prompts, or activities to help them achieve a specific goal. The outline for a workbook often mirrors a step-by-step process or a series of themes. For example, if your workbook is about personal growth, you might organize it into sections like "Discovering Your Values," "Setting Goals," and "Building Daily Habits." Each chapter could include short lessons, followed by exercises with examples, and space for reflection. A workbook's success lies in its actionable format, so think of it as a conversation between you and the reader, where they do the work on the page while your voice guides them and inspires them along the way.

Memoirs are personal, emotional, and deeply reflective. They often cover not the whole life, but a period, event, or theme in the author's life, emphasizing personal experiences, emotions, and reflections. For example, a memoir about overcoming adversity might begin with a pivotal event, explore the struggles that followed, and conclude with lessons learned. It isn't likely to hold events from an entire lifetime (technically that would be an autobiography), but just the ones that revealed the *aha* moments. Alternatively, a thematic memoir could focus on a specific relationship, career path, or life-defining journey, like Cheryl Strayed's *Wild*. Each chapter should build on the last, creating a narrative arc that takes readers on a journey through your experiences. Remember, a memoir isn't just about your life; it's about the universal truths your own unique story reveals.

Personally, I don't love memoirs with writing prompts or a built-in workbook. If I'm deep in reading, I don't want that experience to be interrupted. If you are thinking about adding exercises and prompts to any book, consider how they will impact the reader experience and whether they should be built into the structure, like at the end of chapters or even at the end of the book, or if they should be in a separate workbook altogether.

Business books establish your expertise and provide readers with strategies or frameworks they can implement. These books often start by finding a problem and positioning you as the authority with the solution. A typical outline might include sections like "Understanding the Problem," "Case Studies or Examples," and "Your Proven Framework." For instance, in a book about leadership, you might structure chapters around key leadership principles like communication, delegation, and vision. Each chapter could open with a story or example, dive into the principle, and close with actionable takeaways for the reader.

How-to books are all about delivering value by teaching readers a skill or solving a problem. They follow a clear, straightforward structure. For example, a book on starting a garden could have chapters like "Planning Your Garden," "Choosing the Right Plants," and "Maintaining Your Space." Each chapter should include step-by-step instructions, helpful tips, and possibly visuals or diagrams to enhance understanding. Self-help books focus on inspiring readers and giving actionable advice for personal development. These books often blend storytelling with practical strategies. An outline might begin with "The Problem," move to "Understanding the Challenges," and progress to "Actionable Solutions." Each chapter could address a specific hurdle the reader faces, supported by anecdotes and strategies to overcome it. Books like Brené Brown's *Daring Greatly* combine personal stories, to connect emotionally, and research-backed insights that provide tools for change.

Key Concepts

Remember, this is a working document; you are likely to change it and move things around. It's a tool to get you started. Some of you will know exactly what you plan to write and how it's going to be structured while others may need some refining. Those who work well with outlines will do that, but what if you aren't an outliner? Or what if you aren't ready for that part? Just keep writing until you feel the urge to get organized!

Here are some ideas for streamlining your approach. You may use each or any combination of techniques to help you get on your way.

Approach 1: Find the Top Five Things You Want Readers to Know

List the core ideas, lessons, or insights you want readers to take away. These could be any number of things. Consider the following as prompts:

- Steps they can follow.
- Habits they can adopt.
- Mindset shifts that will change their perspective.

Examples:

- How to embrace feedback without fear.
- The importance of self-reflection in personal growth.
- Building resilience through storytelling.
- Navigating rejection and criticism with grace.

- Turning setbacks into opportunities for transformation.

Approach 2: Decide the Structure

Decide how your key points will fit together. Do they fall into any of these?

- Steps in a process?
- Independent ideas that build on one another?
- Concepts tied together by a central theme?

Example:

- If your ideas are steps, order them in the sequence readers should follow.
- If they are habits, group them by category (e.g., habits for clarity, habits for resilience).
- For mindset shifts, arrange them from foundational concepts to advanced strategies.

Approach 3: Reflect on Your Story

Think about your personal journey and how it relates to your message. Consider the following general questions:

- What pain points or challenges did you face?
- How did you overcome them?
- What transformations have you experienced that can inspire your readers?

Example:

- Share a story of how embracing feedback transformed your own work.
- Include anecdotes about lessons learned from rejection or failure.
- Use personal milestones to illustrate the concepts you're teaching.

Approach 4: Clarify Your Purpose and Message

Write a vision statement for your book that summarizes its purpose. Then distill the main message into two or three concise sentences. Identify key words that will resonate with your target audience.

Example:

- **Vision:** This book empowers readers to embrace growth by learning from feedback and overcoming self-doubt.
- **Message:** Personal growth begins with shifting your mindset. By using feedback as a tool, you can turn challenges into opportunities and achieve your potential.
- **Keywords:** Growth, resilience, mindset, transformation, feedback.

Approach 5: Create the Outline

Organize the content into chapters or sections based on your top three to five points, personal stories, and supporting insights.

- What three to five problems? What examples?
- How attainable are the methods, habits, and steps that will solve the reader's problems? What examples/case studies can I provide the reader with?
- How can I convey my message for the solution in the most manageable way? What examples? Who will agree to share their stories of having used my approach?

It's worth repeating: Once you have experience writing, you will know what approach will work best for you right now. Don't count on a singular approach to work forever; we change when circumstances and environments change.

Approach 6: Start with the End in Mind

Remember how I stated that starting with the end in mind might help you stay focused? Ask yourself: What transformation or takeaway do I want my readers to experience?

This will guide the structure of the book.

Example Goal:

Help readers learn how to effectively embrace feedback to improve their personal and professional lives.

If this end-in-mind approach resonates with you, it may be helpful to divide the book into three main parts, then fill in the prospective chapters or subject headings as below. Nonfiction books often work well when divided into three sections:

1. **The Problem:** What challenges or issues are readers facing?

2. **The Solution:** What methods, habits, or steps will solve the problem?

3. **The Application:** How can readers apply these solutions in real life?

While some of this may seem repetitive, my hope is that I've restated it in a way that aligns with you, resonates with you, or I've said it in a way that truly lands with who you are and your approach to discovering your next best steps.

If you like having templates to work from, try this:

Nonfiction Book Outline Template

Title:

Subtitle:

Introduction:

Start with a compelling story, fact, or question that draws the reader in. Clearly explain what the book is about and why it's relevant to the reader. Outline what the reader will gain or learn by reading this book. Share why you're the right person to write this book and your personal connection to the topic.

Part 1: Understanding the Problem

Define the main issue or challenge your book addresses. Share relatable examples or statistics to illustrate its importance. Explore the underlying causes or factors contributing to the problem and provide context or historical background if relevant. Show how this issue affects the reader or their world by including personal anecdotes, case studies, or data to make it tangible.

Part 2: Implementing the Solution

Introduce the first actionable step or concept the reader needs to address the problem. Include exercises, tips, or reflection prompts to guide the reader. Expand on the first step, diving deeper into strategies or methods, and providing examples of success stories or practical applications. Address common challenges or roadblocks readers might face, offering solutions or mindset shifts to help them stay on track.

Part 3: Living the Solution

Show how readers can integrate the principles or strategies into their daily routines. Emphasize the ongoing benefits of applying what they've learned and offer advice on sustaining momentum and adapting the solutions over time. Include inspiring examples of people who've succeeded using your framework or ideas.

Conclusion

Reinforce the main points covered in the book. Encourage readers to take the next step or implement what they've learned. End with an uplifting message or vision for the reader's future.

Extras (Optional Sections)

You may include worksheets, templates, or tools for readers to download or use. Consider adding a section to address frequently asked questions or common concerns readers might have. You might use an acknowledgments section to thank individuals or groups who contributed to your book and provide references or a further reading list for readers who want to dive deeper into the topic.

None of this will happen without your daily, committed practice of writing. Reading this book, taking a course, and attending online workshops will not create the book. Writing will.

Daily writing doesn't mean you need to write chapters every day. It's about building a habit. It's about committing to and showing up for self. Even if you write for just fifteen minutes a day, it's the habit that counts. By committing to this, you'll see steady progress over time. What if you have a lifestyle that allows you to only write on weekends or specific days of the week? That's okay too; just make sure you are reinforcing the habit. For some, personal habits and routine is enough; for others, accountability is needed.

Create accountability by joining a writing group or setting weekly goals, then showing up and posting your word count/time on task. Sharing your progress with others can help maintain motivation and keep you on track. Having a visual tracker can help.

Some writers thrive on daily habits, while others write in bursts. It's important to find your rhythm, whether that's committing to a few minutes every day or setting aside larger blocks of time when you're most focused. Both approaches can lead to success. The key is understanding what works best for you without feeling pressured to follow someone else's routine.

In our writers' group, we meet once a week for dedicated writing sessions. This regular writing time helps establish a routine and ensures you are consistently making progress. It's also kind of nice to have others writing at the same time, together but separate. It can remind you that you are not alone.

The key is finding your rhythm and sticking to it, knowing there's no one right way to do it. Find your flow. Be disciplined. Be open to flexibility but have deadlines. You'll need both.

Now, the fun (and work) has begun. Editing, refining, and shaping your manuscript will bring it closer to what you've dreamed it could be. But for now, celebrate this moment. A first draft is a huge accomplishment, and it's the first big step in turning your vision into reality.

First Draft

The Parts of a Book

When you're working on your first draft, the goal is to create the foundation of your book. You'll be rewriting and editing, but you'll have something tangible to build upon. It's helpful to start thinking about the structure and elements that will eventually make up the complete manuscript. Let's walk through what goes into a first draft and the pieces you'll need to address.

1. Introduction or Preface

Your introduction is where you welcome readers into your world and set the tone for the book. This can be a short introduction, a preface explaining why you wrote the book or a personal story connecting you to the topic. It doesn't have to be perfect right now—capture your thoughts about how you want to communicate with your reader and establish the book's purpose. Consider these questions to help you get started.

- Why did you write this book?
- What should the reader expect?
- How does this book fit into a reader's life or solve their problem?

2. Front Matter

The front matter consists of all the elements that come before your main content. While it may not feel like a priority in the early stages, having placeholders for these sections can sometimes make things easier later. If this feels like minutia and you want to cut to the guts of the book, skim right over this. Common elements of books:

- **Title Page:** Your book's title, subtitle (if you have one), and your name.
- **Dedication (optional):** If you want to dedicate the book to someone, make a note of it here.
- **Acknowledgments (optional):** Jot down names or groups of people you might want to thank.
- **Table of Contents:** This doesn't need to be detailed yet, but having an outline of your chapters may help with structure.

3. Chapter Breaks

Deciding where your chapters begin and end is part of the drafting process. Don't overthink this in the first draft but do try to organize your content into logical chunks or themes. Even if you're not sure about the exact flow yet, inserting clean page or section breaks will make revising easier. Use placeholders like "Chapter 1: [Title Here]" to give your draft some order.

4. Main Content

The heart of your book is, of course, the main content. This is where you'll pour your ideas, stories, and knowledge onto the page. Focus on the message you want to convey in each chapter. Remember:

- It doesn't have to be in perfect order right now.
- Write freely, and don't get bogged down by trying to edit as you go.
- If you feel stuck, use writing prompts or questions to keep the words flowing.

5. Page Breaks

While drafting, use clear page breaks between sections and chapters. These are placeholders that make navigating your manuscript easier for both you and your editors, and eventually, your future readers. Many writing programs allow you to insert these breaks automatically, so take advantage of that feature.

6. Spellcheck and Grammar

A first draft doesn't have to be edited, but it's a good idea to run whatever options your program offers to catch obvious errors. Typos and grammar mistakes are expected at this stage, so don't stress about seeing every one of them, just aim to make your writing readable.

7. Notes and Placeholders

Create a note as a reminder to work on a section later. If you aren't ready to write or there will be research you need to do, add a placeholder. For example:

- [Insert statistics here.]
- [Write story about the workshop in 2018.]

These notes will remind you what needs to be filled in later, allowing you to keep writing without losing momentum. By putting brackets around what you want to insert, you can search and easily find what you are looking for.

8. Resources, For Further Reading, Other

This won't be necessary in all books. If you cited statistics and studies, you would need to keep careful documentation of where you found them and would need to create a bibliography of sorts. The same goes for quotes you have pulled from your favorite books and sites. If you aren't sure what is in the public domain and what needs permission to reprint, it's a great idea to keep careful track of the sources anyway so your editors can help you figure out the copyright information.

Keep a running list if you have favorite movies, books, channels, sites, or podcasts that may also help the reader. It's easier to do this as you go instead of trying to brainstorm your favorites when you are well past this stage. Make sure you have a disclaimer that web and online sources can change, and you aren't responsible for outdated links or references.

Okay, so you've put together what feels like your first draft. What happens next? It is now ready to go to a developmental editor. As mentioned, you should have run programs to fix glaring errors, but don't worry about whether the book is ready to publish—it won't be! It will go through at least one and probably two or three rounds of editing, including adding words, cutting words, and sometimes changing the order of chapters.

This is your *first* draft. Don't be too attached to it.

Having a first draft manuscript is a significant milestone, but it's just that—a draft. It's messy, imperfect, and full of possibilities.

When you have a first draft, it means you've shown up, you've written through the doubts, distractions, and everything else that tries to get in your way. You've done what so many people talk about but never actually do—you've written a book.

A first draft is also a chance to really see what's working and what's not. It's where you start to notice the themes, the strengths, and the gaps. It might not (yet) be the book you envision, but it holds the essence of your message and your purpose.

And here's the truth: No one's first draft is perfect. The first draft is about courage, not perfection. It's about honoring your creativity and allowing the words to flow without judgment.

When you're holding your first draft, whether it's printed out or still on your laptop, it's a testament to your commitment. It's proof that you're serious about sharing your message and story with the world.

After the Draft—Moving to Publishing

Editors

Oh! It's time to share your writing. Don't panic. Every author goes through a moment of impostor syndrome or feeling they will be judged for their writing. It's normal, and you have to work through those feelings and send it off!

There are several types of editors, each playing a unique role in the publishing process. We work with developmental editors, beta readers (not technically editors, but will give feedback), copy editors, and then proofreaders.

The first editor you'll need is your bird's-eye view, a developmental editor who will work with your first draft to organize and provide feedback. They may give you tips and tidbits for improving your book's flow. They will suggest you cut, rewrite, move, and add to that first draft. Once you and the developmental editor feel good about your working manuscript, beta readers are selected to read and give feedback from a first-time reader's view. These first readers play a crucial role in helping you identify your manuscript's strengths, uncover areas that need more clarity, and ensure your ideas align with your vision. Their feedback provides a fresh perspective, offering insights you might not have considered, and serves as a foundation for taking your draft to the next level. Working with them is not just about refining your book, it's about building confidence in your writing and gaining the tools you need to bring your story or message to life.

Developmental editors focus on the big picture, helping you refine your book's structure, flow, and overall content. They guide you in shaping your ideas, ensuring your message is clear and impactful.

Line editors dive into the nuances of your writing, polishing sentence structure, tone, and style to enhance readability and consistency.

Copy editors concentrate on grammar, punctuation, and technical accuracy, ensuring your manuscript is error free.

Finally, proofreaders are the last set of eyes before publication, catching any remaining typos or formatting issues.

Each type of editor brings invaluable expertise and a unique perspective to your book, working together to help your manuscript shine.

Working with editors is a collaborative process that transforms a manuscript from good to great. An editor brings fresh eyes, professional ability, and a deep understanding of what makes writing resonate with readers. They help refine your message, strengthen your voice, and ensure your ideas flow seamlessly. While it can feel vulnerable to share your work, partnering with the right editor at the right time is a powerful step toward creating a polished, impactful book. They're not there to rewrite your words or change your voice but to amplify your vision, helping you present your ideas in the clearest, most compelling, way possible.

Remember, the first draft might have some errors, repeated sentences or ideas, and maybe even missing chapters—and that's okay. It's a first draft. Many authors get tired of writing and organizing and take this opportunity to send their manuscript to an editor for a first read-through. Whether you review your book yourself or have an editor do it, this is the stage to look for missing pieces, assess the book's flow, and ensure it's in the right order. We're still not focusing on refining sentence structure—yet. It's just a first read-through.

You can work with one editor who will take your book all the way through to proofing or work with several editors. This is where the power of an editing team comes in. Editing is your friend, not your enemy. During editing, your ideas become clear, the rough edges of your writing are smoothed out, and the story truly begins to shine.

Look at the big picture first—structure, pacing, and flow before diving into the details. Each draft brings the manuscript closer to its best version, but perfection is never the goal. It's about improving the manuscript with each round of edits, turning a good draft into a great book.

Embracing Feedback

As writers, we often work in isolation, pouring our hearts and souls onto the page without any outside input. However, seeking feedback on our work can be one of the most valuable steps we can take before publishing. Choose the right people to give you feedback. I don't recommend asking your best friend or spouse or sibling. You want someone who would enjoy reading your book, understand what type of feedback you need, and it's also crucial that they recognize your goals. You don't want someone telling you that they don't like potatoes and would never follow your potato diet. You are looking for feedback that answers questions you'll ask. Finding readers involves reaching out to people who represent your target audience and can provide honest, constructive feedback. Your first readers might be a trusted friend, former boss, coach, or someone who loves books and believes in you. These are the early eyes on your draft—the people you trust to offer thoughtful encouragement and gentle honesty.

While your editor will provide professional feedback later, there's something powerful about having someone read your raw work. If they love it, they might even become your first endorser.

Choose just one or two people to start. Don't ask too many, and don't ask too early. Look for someone who can say, "This part really works" and also help you see what's missing or unclear, without crushing your confidence. Here's where tapping into writing groups, online forums, and social media communities may be helpful in order to connect with potential beta readers. Be sure to choose individuals who can offer objective insights and are willing to dedicate time to your manuscript. If you get stuck, reach out. These first readers are not the same as beta readers. Beta happens when you are close to publishing but need first-time readers to weigh in on how you can tighten the book up.

Feedback can happen at any time and can be from reading chunks, sections, chapters, or a whole first draft. Once the first draft is ready for next steps, that's when you can get someone to help you see if you need developmental help or if you can go to line/copy editing. At GracePoint, we send manuscripts to beta after the developmental edits are complete.

GracePoint prepares a PDF of your manuscript to send to beta readers. These readers are asked specific questions, and those questions may be more pointed than the feedback you ask from a friend on an especially tough chapter you wrote. Beta feedback helps the author and the publishing team see a first-time reader's perspective of something that the author and the editor both know intimately. Sometimes you can't see the forest for the trees, so this feedback is crucial.

Michelle A. Vandepas

General Questions GracePoint Asks Beta Readers

1. Did the book hold your interest from start to finish? If not, where did it lose you?

2. Were there any parts of the book that felt confusing or unclear?

3. What did you enjoy most about the book?

4. Did any part of the book feel repetitive or unnecessary?

Content and Clarity

1. Were the main ideas and themes clear throughout the book?

2. Were there areas where you wanted more explanation or detail?

3. Did you notice any gaps in the content, such as missing sections or unanswered questions?

Structure and Flow

1. Did the book feel well-organized? Were there any sections that felt out of place?

2. Did the transitions between chapters or sections feel smooth?

3. Was the pacing appropriate? Did any parts feel too rushed or too slow?

Tone and Voice

1. Did the tone feel consistent throughout the book?

2. Did the author's voice resonate with you? If not, what felt off?

Audience Connection

1. Did the book feel like it was written for its intended audience?

2. Were there any sections that felt too technical or oversimplified?

3. Did the book address the questions or problems it promised to solve?

Emotional Impact

1. Were there any moments that made you feel particularly inspired or connected to the material?

2. Did the book feel relatable or relevant to your own experiences?

3. Were there any moments that felt emotionally flat or disengaging?

Final Impressions

1. If you had to describe the book in one sentence, what would you say?

2. Would you recommend this book to others? Why or why not?

3. Do you have any other suggestions or comments for improvement?

GracePoint then takes this feedback and organizes it for you; if you are working with an editor, ask them to do it for you. Sometimes you get opposing points of view and you'll need a discerning eye to understand what you might change or know! Another thing to remember is that if you ask ten people, you may get ten different avenues for suggested improvement. Here's where working with experienced professionals can help.

Here's an example: Imagine you have written a memoir, and you have left out a very important traumatic event that you know shaped the positioning of you career choice. You intentionally left it out because you didn't want to "go there." Your

Michelle A. Vandepas

editor has suggested that it feels like something important has been left out, and you stick with your mental stance: *I can't go there*. You are wrestling with whether you think it's really that obvious that it's been omitted, and you write a version that includes it, but you keep it for yourself. When you send your manuscript to beta, your readers ask the same question: "Did you leave something out? It feels like a big story is missing." You are still the author, and you can still choose to include that story or not, but the editor gently reveals that all these people also felt there was a missing piece. This might help you decide if it's worth putting in or not.

Here's another example about choosing the right readers: Things change rapidly and with greater research, right? The fields of quantum mechanics and epigenetics are revealing new understandings of these systems each day. Imagine asking your retired seventh grade science teacher to give feedback on your book based on cutting edge science when they have not kept up with contemporary research. Imagine the feedback you could get if they still think these are far-fetched theories. Your editor will help with that.

Take some time to consider each piece of feedback carefully and decide which suggestions will help make your work stronger.

And please, don't take all criticism at face value. Sometimes readers' opinions are subjective or based on personal preferences rather than something inherently *wrong* with your writing. If you ask someone who only reads fantasy to give you feedback on your self-help book, you may not get valuable constructive criticism. In this situation, use your judgment when deciding which changes to make and which ones don't align with your vision for the piece.

Another way to use feedback constructively is by looking for patterns in multiple critiques. If several people mention similar issues with your story, there may be something there worth exploring further. On the other hand, if only one person suggests a change that doesn't resonate with others who have read it, then perhaps it's not as crucial as it seemed to that person.

Finally, remember that while receiving constructive criticism can be challenging at times, using this tool will help you as a writer and will improve the final product. Accepting another perspective on your work through others' eyes makes you more aware of potential flaws in your writing style, allowing you to grow into a better writer overall.

Try not to be triggered, upset, or crushed by feedback. It's just that—feedback—and it's your book, your writing, your vision. Use the feedback as a tool and as inspiration to keep making your book better! This is one of the stretching opportunities!

Your First Endorsers

Don't Freak Out!

Writing a book is about more than just putting words on a page. It's about stepping into your purpose, claiming your voice, and creating something that can impact others in meaningful ways, and all of this will help you level up yourself and stretch you beyond your current ideas. Writing your book is about putting your stake in the ground and standing up for your voice.

This book has been about more than guidance; it's been about encouraging you to take bold steps toward your goals. Whether you're writing to share your expertise, tell your story, or inspire others, the tools and strategies here are designed to support you not just in completing your book, but in understanding the deeper purpose behind it.

Remember, your book is not just a project, it's a conversation with the world. You've clarified your ideas, found your audience, and begun to craft something that reflects your unique voice and message. By doing so, you've stepped into the role of an author, a thought leader, and a changemaker.

As you move forward, stay connected to your why. Keep asking yourself: *Who am I writing for? What impact do I want this book to have?* These answers will guide you through the next phases of writing, editing, and publishing, keeping you aligned with the purpose that brought you here in the first place.

Finally, trust that your story, your expertise, and your voice are needed. There is someone out there who needs to hear what you have to share, and by showing up on the page, you are creating the ripple effect that will inspire and transform. You've already taken the first step—now, keep going.

This is the stage where you might go into panic. *Now what? Am I worthy? Yikes, I'm exposed.*

It's okay.

This is your journey, and the world is waiting for your words.

Final Thoughts

You've made it this far, which means your book still matters to you. So, here's the deal: You either write it or you don't. But don't pretend it doesn't matter anymore. You don't need permission. You don't need to wait. And you definitely don't need to get it right on the first try. You just need to write. Because your message won't wait forever—and the people who need your book are already out there.

If I can go from being humiliated at fifteen to writing several books, you can too. You don't have to know everything before you start. It's okay to write for visibility, legacy, business—or simply because you feel the nudge and don't know why yet.

Let it be creative, messy, healing, and fun. You don't need a perfect reason—just a willingness to begin.

Your words matter. To you. To someone else. Maybe to many people. So write. And let me know how it's going.

Afterthoughts
(after writing)

My Thoughts on Publishing

Whether you self-publish, go hybrid, land a traditional deal, or something in between, those decisions come later.

Right now, you don't need to know every option. You just need to write the book.

That's the hard part. Not picking the printer. Not choosing a cover. Not even marketing. It's writing. And there's no shortcut.

I've done all types of publishing and everything keeps changing. I don't know which way *you* should go yet, but I know I can help you navigate and discern the right path for you.

As you go through these steps, I wish for you to deeply think about each of these questions before you choose how to publish. A great publisher has expertise in these areas and will help you complete all the steps while evaluating and giving feedback as you go. If you'd like to explore working with GracePoint Publishing or myself, reach out. We know how to really hold you and your message as something sacred. We do not see you or your book as just a commodity or something to sell. We see you as a human being with a message that's important and needs to be shared with the world. You have something to say, something important to share. Let's get it out there.

The journey from first draft to manuscript to a published book is both exhilarating and complex. Before diving in, there are essential aspects every author should carefully evaluate to ensure their vision aligns with the practicalities of publishing. From royalties to foreign rights, editing to marketing, here are key points to guide your decisions.

Whether you're polishing your manuscript or thinking about distribution, every step requires careful consideration. Here are things to reflect on before diving into publishing.

One of the first things to consider is how your book's concept and structure will come together. Do you need help refining your ideas or narrowing your focus? A good publishing partner will offer collaborative brainstorming sessions and guidance during the early stages to clarify your vision and set a strong foundation. This is particularly important for first-time authors who may feel overwhelmed by their many ideas.

Once your manuscript is complete, the review and editing processes become vital. It's essential to understand how your manuscript will be reviewed and what kind of feedback you'll receive. Will it cover structure, pacing, and concept development? Does the process include multiple rounds of editing, such as developmental, line, and copy editing? What about beta readers and proofreading? Keep in mind that each publishing approach has positive aspects and potential pitfalls, and there certainly is no one-size-fits-all. It's important to know where you stand as the writer in whatever agreement you enter into. For example, if the company provides editing as part of their deal, what kind of editing is it? How many rounds? Will the editing process be collaborative, or will you be expected to accept every change? Do you keep any involvement in or control over your words?

And what if you have decided to go the self-publishing route? Have you checked the prices for everything? And how does one find qualified people to help with each of the steps to creating a book? Many self-publishers simply take what you have and viola, it's a book. There's no polishing, no developing, no editing, no proofing, no opportunities for marketing, no cover design. For some companies, you have to supply all of this. This can prove to be cost-prohibitive for many as each step outlined here will have individual costs you may not have planned for. You may hate the whole process of managing this. Keep that in mind as you read forward.

Polishing your manuscript each step of the way not only elevates its quality but also ensures it will resonate with readers while staying true to your voice.

Beyond the content, the presentation of your book is just as critical. A compelling cover design can draw readers in, while a clean and professional interior layout ensures an enjoyable reading experience. Consider whether the publisher involves you in the design process to create a cover that reflects your book's message and whether they pay attention to interior details like typography, spacing, and visuals. These seemingly small elements can make a big difference.

What categories will your book fit into? How competitive are they? Are your categories saturated? These are questions you will want to discuss with your publisher so that you accurately categorize your work.

Another important step is securing the legal and technical components of your book. Will your publisher handle obtaining an ISBN, Library of Congress Control Number (LCCN), and copyright? Proper cataloging ensures your book is officially recognized, while copyright protection safeguards your intellectual property. Make sure these details are clearly outlined in any agreements you sign.

Distribution is a key factor in your book's success. Ask about where your book will be sold—will it be available in physical stores, online retailers, or both? Is it going to be print on demand? Additionally, explore whether the publisher has connections to libraries, independent bookstores, and international markets. Broad distribution is essential to reach a diverse audience and maximize your book's impact.

Marketing and promotion are areas where many authors need extra support. An effective publisher will help craft a marketing plan that includes social media, promotional materials, and launch events. Some may even aid with securing media appearances or collaborations with influencers. Remember, good marketing doesn't just sell books, it builds your brand as an author and connects you with your audience.

Another aspect to consider is how your publishing partner manages rights and adaptations. Who will retain the rights to potential audiobooks, film adaptations, or translations? A good publisher should be experienced in managing these opportunities and negotiating deals for foreign markets. This opens doors for your book to reach audiences beyond your immediate market.

Financial transparency is another critical factor. Before signing any contract, ensure you understand how royalties are calculated and when payments will be made. Does the publisher provide a royalty dashboard or similar tool to track sales and earnings? These features not only build trust but also empower you to make strategic decisions for your book and career.

Production and inventory management are equally important. Will the publisher handle print quantities and shipping logistics? Ask how they manage stock to avoid overproduction or shortages. Efficient inventory systems keep your book accessible to readers without creating unnecessary costs.

If you're considering an audiobook version of your book, explore whether the publisher offers audio production services.

Many authors find audiobooks to be a valuable addition to their publishing strategy, reaching new audiences and increasing overall sales. Ensure your publishing partner can connect you with professional voice talent or guide you through the recording process.

Last, think about what happens after the launch. Publishing a book is just one key step of your journey. Will your publisher provide long-term support and resources for your next project? Some may even help with continued author branding and strategies to maintain momentum. This kind of ongoing partnership can be invaluable as you grow as an author.

By reflecting on these considerations and asking the right questions, you'll be better prepared to navigate the publishing process. Each decision shapes the future of your book, so choose a publishing partner who aligns with your vision and values. With the right support, you can confidently bring your book to life and connect with readers in meaningful ways.

Questions to Ask When Reviewing Publishers

General Publishing Services

- How will you support me in refining and completing my book's concept and outline?
- Do you offer sessions to help me clarify my vision and align it with market needs?
- How accessible will an editing or coaching team be throughout the process?

Manuscript Review and Editing

- What is your process for developmental editing, and how collaborative is it? How many rounds?
- Do you provide multiple rounds of edits, including copy editing and proofreading?
- At what stage in the process do you have test readers (beta)?
- How do you ensure my voice and style remain intact throughout the editing process?

Design and Layout

- Can I review and provide input during the cover design process?
- How will the interior layout of my book be optimized for both print and digital formats?

- What trends in design are you considering for books in my genre?

Legal and Administrative Support

- How do you manage ISBN registration and Library of Congress Control Number acquisition?
- How will my intellectual property be protected under your publishing model?

Distribution

- Where will my book be distributed, and how extensive is your retail and library network?
- Do you have partnerships with international distributors or niche retailers?
- In what ways am I expected to be involved (if at all) in distribution? How can I access books to sell at events that I set up independently?

Marketing and Promotion

- What specific marketing strategies do you implement to promote books?
- What are the steps to create a detailed marketing plan tailored to my book and audience?
- How involved are you in organizing launch events or virtual campaigns for authors?

Foreign and Audiobook Rights

- How will you help negotiate and manage foreign rights for translations?
- What if I want to create or distribute an audiobook version of my book? How does that work?

Royalties and Financial Transparency

- How are royalties calculated, and how often are payments issued?

- Do you provide tools like a royalty dashboard to track sales and earnings?
- How can I track the daily/weekly sales of my book?

Feedback and Collaboration

- Do you work with developmental editors? Will I receive structured feedback from them?
- What about line and copy editors?
- At what stage of the process are beta readers called upon? How does that work?
- How do you handle author reviews and sign-offs at various stages of the process?

Post-Publication Support

- What kind of long-term support can I expect after my book's release?
- Are there additional services available for branding and marketing my future projects?

General Experience and Flexibility

- How do you ensure a personalized experience tailored to my book's needs?
- Can I select specific services, or it is an all-inclusive package?

GracePoint Publishing

After being a publishing consultant for fifteen years, I co-founded GracePoint Publishing and am now the owner and publisher. I've learned a lot since I started publishing in 2014, and I consider us a bespoke premier publishing house for leaders, teachers, and creatives like you. We are devoted to helping our clients accelerate and amplify their impact, information transmission, and inspiration.

We understand that traditional book publishing represents only a fraction of the innovative ways information and creativity can be shared with the world. Our company is collaborative and can also help you with speaking on stages, podcasting, creating online content for classes and programs, magazines, blogs, audiobooks, and who knows what else! Whatever it is, we want to help you share your message with the world!

Our clients are connected to a sense of purpose, meaning, and mission. This connection gives them the courage and power to transcend the limitations (and fear) of their old beliefs and egos. They are driven to be leaders, innovators, and disruptors in their field, and (maybe with coaching) they aren't afraid to take *bold* risks in pursuing their purpose and passion.

We are collaborative and work with our authors to write, polish, and promote their books, their message, and their work in the world. We know exactly what it takes to get your book and your message out into the world.

Michelle A. Vandepas

We have an in-house group of talented and committed people who help you best by understanding your purpose, your book's mission, and your message. Our attentive publishing team takes the time to really feel into what you envision with your book, then they carefully assist you each step of the way, handing you off to the next person in the process, and always explaining where the steps are headed and what to expect.

Sometimes, authors come to us with a complete manuscript. We are happy to help evaluate the manuscript for next steps. Maybe it's ready, maybe it needs some editing. As I've often said, I won't let you publish crap!

Some authors come to us with half-formed collections of thoughts, of false starts, or of many pages of writing without clear direction. They are stuck, and they need a coach. Our coaches help you release the book from your body, mind, and spirit or simply help you reach a place where the book can flow more easily, as if channeling it from that higher part of you. Sometimes our developmental editors do the coaching, and sometimes, our publishing leaders coach.

If you're stuck, short on time, or want a guide at your side, a ghostwriter might be the perfect fit. A great ghost preserves your voice and message—it's still your book, just with support.

I've worked with ghostwriters myself. You don't have to write every word alone for it to be authentic.

Whether it's a ghostwriter, a coach, an editor, or an accountability partner, the right help can keep you moving and bring your book to life.

We've all been there—and I've certainly made my share of mistakes and more. As a publisher, I hear the same stories over and over: things authors wish they'd known, or things I wish they'd come to me about sooner. Here are a few of them along with tips to help you avoid these common missteps.

Rushing to Edit Too Early

Oh boy. This is the biggest one I see. Authors come to me so proud they've gotten an edit; however, they paid for a copy edit before looking at the structure and flow of the book. Every book has rewrites, and if you skip that step, you'll end up editing it over and over, wasting time and money and likely getting in the headspace of: *I'm so done with this book. I'm sick of it.*

Try not to edit too much as you go; then when you have a draft, look at the flow. Do the chapters make sense? Are they in the right order? You might need a developmental editor at this stage. But you are not ready for proofreading. Don't rush the process.

Choosing the Wrong Editor

Not all feedback is created equal and choosing someone who doesn't understand your vision or genre can be frustrating. You need someone who "gets" your book and can offer insights that align with your goals. Be intentional about who you trust with your manuscript—it's your story, and it deserves the right kind of support. When you are ready for an editor, understand what stage you are in.

I suggest working with a book coach or developmental editor after a first draft (or if you need help getting to the first draft). At this stage, it's about the flow of the book, the content, and the structure. What are the key takeaways, and how should they be included in stories? This is not copy editing or spelling. This is a very high-level look at the book.

Go into rewrites and organization (or reorganization) before you move to the next steps.

Having Someone Read Your Work Too Early

Sharing your work before you've had a chance to fully refine your thoughts can be counterproductive. Early feedback on ideas that aren't yet fully formed may feel overwhelming or unhelpful. Give yourself time to shape your vision and clarify your message before inviting others to read it.

I'm a gardener. I plant tiny little tomato seedlings in tiny little pots and put them in my windowsill, allowing them to enjoy sunlight before planting them out into the big windy hot garden.

Don't share your work before it has roots—before it can withstand the harsh climate of editors, beta readers, and early reviewers. Hold your work closely.

And then when it's time, release it (like parents release teenagers).

Ignoring Feedback

It's easy to dismiss feedback that doesn't feel right, especially if it stings a little. But sometimes, the best insights come from sitting with those critiques and considering how they could strengthen your book. You don't have to take every piece of advice, but looking for patterns in feedback can uncover ways to make your work even better. At this stage, it's all about asking the right questions and in the right way. Ask open-ended question. For example, change "Did you like my book?" to "Which chapter was your favorite and why?" Change "Did my book inspire you?" to "What was your biggest takeaway from my book?" Change "Does my book need more editing?" to "Which chapter needs the most work? Be specific."

My publishing company has a specific process for early readers.

Taking Feedback Too Personally

Feedback is about the work, not about you. It can feel vulnerable to share your writing, but critiques aren't an attack on your abilities—they're opportunities to grow. Try to approach feedback with curiosity and see it as a partnership to make your book shine.

Skipping the Feedback Process

Fear of criticism can keep you from sharing your work, but feedback is how your book grows. Choose trusted readers or editors who can help you refine your ideas and strengthen your message. Their insights are invaluable.

Underestimating the Time Needed for Revisions

Revising takes time. It's not just a quick polish but a process of refining your ideas, tightening your structure, and making sure everything flows. Don't rush it. Each round of revisions brings you closer to a finished book you can be proud of.

Ignoring Structure and Flow

Even the best ideas can get lost if they're not organized well. Make sure your book has a clear structure that guides readers through your message. Think of it as creating a path for them to follow.

Neglecting the Emotional Impact

Readers want more than just information, they want to feel connected to your story. Don't be afraid to share emotions, struggles, and triumphs. The heart of your book is what will resonate most. Add stories, examples, and take your readers on the journey with you.

Not Taking Care of Yourself

Writing can take a toll if you're not mindful of your own needs. Skipping meals, losing sleep, or burning out won't help your creativity. Make self-care a priority—it's what keeps you energized and focused.

Writing When You're Not Ready

If you're processing a significant loss or emotional event, it's okay to pause. Journal and reflect, but don't feel pressured to dive into a manuscript before you're ready. Your story will still be there when the time is right. When I talk with authors who have gone through traumas or large life changes, like illness, death, and divorce I recommend starting with journaling, then waiting at least two years before drafting the book. You need perspective. Your book will change as you get distance.

Failing to Celebrate Milestones

Every step in the writing journey is worth celebrating. Whether it's finishing a chapter, completing your first draft, or surviving revisions, take time to honor your progress. Writing a book is no small feat—you deserve to recognize how far you've come.

Relying (Too Much) on AI

While it may be tempting to take your structure and use one of the many rapidly growing platforms for artificially generated information, we recommend that this be used minimally and *only* to help you get unstuck. If you have used any version of AI, be sure to use your own personal editing skills to make it sound, well, less artificial. Only you as a human have the passion needed to articulate exactly what you want to say to your audience. Trust that over AI.

These thoughts are not meant to scare you or stop you; they are simply to alert you that when you hit a speed bump, it doesn't mean you abandon the vehicle or trip. It just means that this is yet another "normal" thing that may happen through the writing process.

Final Thoughts

You've come this far, and that means something. Whether you're holding a rough draft, scattered notes, or a solid manuscript, you've said yes to yourself and your message. Writing a book isn't about being perfect—it's about being brave. It's about trusting that your voice matters, your story is worthy, and your ideas have a place in the world. Keep going. Keep writing. You don't need permission. You just need to keep showing up for yourself, one word at a time. And if no one has told you lately: I'm proud of you. You're a writer.

If you'd like next steps, I've included a few recourses for you. I'd be honored if you'd join me at a retreat, online workshop or just to connect. If you'd like to find out more about writing and publishing, reach out. My team and I would love to hear from you.

Most of all. Don't give up on your dreams. They matter

Resources

While there is no way to address all the tools that are out there to help a person stay on task for writing, here are just a few I can confidently recommend because I use them. You will find your own way, but don't let the "how" get in the way. At this stage, you just want to write, write, and write some more.

Scrivener

- A powerful tool for organizing your manuscript, research, and notes in one place. Perfect for longer works like books.
- www.literatureandlatte.com

Google Docs

- Free and user-friendly for writing and collaboration. Its cloud storage ensures you can access your work anywhere.
- docs.google.com

Grammarly

- An AI-powered proofreading tool that helps with grammar, punctuation, and clarity.
- www.grammarly.com

ProWritingAid

- A comprehensive editing tool that offers grammar checks, style suggestions, and readability improvements.
- Prowritingaid.com

My favorite books for authors

1. On Writing: A Memoir of the Craft by Stephen King

    - A blend of memoir and master class on writing.

2. Bird by Bird: Some Instructions on Writing and Life by Anne Lamott

    - A humorous and practical guide to the writing process.

3. The War of Art: Break Through the Blocks and Win Your Inner Creative Battles by Steven Pressfield

    - A motivational book for overcoming procrastination and self-doubt.

4. Writing Down the Bones: Freeing the Writer Within by Natalie Goldberg

    - A spiritual and practical guide to developing a writing habit.

5. The Artist's Way: A Spiritual Path to Higher Creativity by Julia Cameron

    - A transformative guide to unlocking creativity and overcoming blocks through practical exercises and techniques.

6. The Elements of Style by William Strunk Jr. and E.B. White

    - A classic guide on clear and concise writing.

7. Big Magic: Creative Living Beyond Fear by Elizabeth Gilbert

    - A book on embracing creativity and overcoming fear.

Editors' Picks (In addition to the above)

Never Say You Can't Survive by Charlie Jane Anders

On Writing Well: The Classic Guide to Writing Nonfiction by William Zinsser

Telling Lies for Fun and Profit by Lawrence Block

My resources for you:

Future Reader Meditation:
www.michellevandepas.com/reader-resources

Facebook Author Path group: www.facebook.com/share/g/19NAGFjgCM/?mibextid=wwXlfr

Michelle's TEDx on Procrastination

GracePoint Publishing is a full-service publisher specializing in helping authors refine their message and publish with impact.

Check out our site at: www.GracePointPublishing.com.

For more information on publishing: https://gracepointpublishing.com/connect/

You can also reach me personally at
www.michellecoaches.com
or
www.michellevandepas.com/connect/

About the Author

Michelle Vandepas is an author, TEDx speaker, and business coach, and the co-founder of GracePoint Publishing. Over the past 25 years as a teacher, coach, and speaker, she has worked with thousands of authors, published more than 200 books through her company, and guided another 200 self-published authors to bring their work to the world.

She works with authors of all kinds, specializing in helping coaches, speakers, service professionals, and personal development and healing experts transform their message into a lasting legacy.

Known for her TEDx talk *In Honor of Procrastination*, Michelle Vandepas explores the difference between procrastination and "percolation" (the idea that waiting can allow ideas to mature).

Her upcoming book, *Divine and Dangerous*, will be released in early 2026 and will be available everywhere books are sold.

Learn more at MichelleVandepas.com.

For more great books from Empower Press
Visit Books.GracePointPublishing.com

EMPOWER
P R E S S

If you enjoyed reading *Write Your Dang Book!*, and purchased it through an online retailer, please return to the site and write a review to help others find the book.

www.ingramcontent.com/pod-product-compliance
Lightning Source LLC
Chambersburg PA
CBHW072147090426
42739CB00013B/3304